# Cookbook for the Renal Diet

Change Your Eating Habits for the Better

Felipe J. Clay

# Contents

# Chapter One

# THE RENAL DIET

Was the Renal Diet and how did it work for me?

In patients with impaired or impaired renal capacities or chronic kidney diseases, the renal eating regimen is a dietary regimen that is intended to relieve their symptoms. As we discussed in detail near the end of Chapter 1, there is no single formally dressed type of renal diet. This is because the requirements of renal diet, as well as its limitations, must match the requirements of the patient and be based on what the specialist recommended for the patient's overall health.

However, all types of renal diets function in the same way, which is to improve your renal capacities, provide some assistance to your kidneys, and prevent kidney disease in patients who have a variety of risk factors, while also improving your overall health and well-being in the process.

It is our hope that the fundamental food items we have provided will assist you in determining which basic food items you should incorporate into your eating regimen and which food gatherings should be avoided in order to improve the presentation of your kidneys, allowing you to begin looking for your new way of life right away. You don't have to look for a wide variety of basic food items all of the time because it's always better to use fresh produce, though frozen food can be a good substitute when fresh products from the soil aren't available.

Consider canned goods in the same way that they were in the previous section, and remember to channel any excess liquid from the canned foods. The renal eating regimen that we recommend in our aide is one that provides an answer in the form of low-sodium and low-potassium meals and food, which is why we also provide basic and simple renal eating regimen plans in our aide. If you have any questions, please contact us at [email protected]. We have recorded in our definitive staple rundown for renal patients that by following a dietary arrangement assembled for all phases of renal framework failure, except if the specialist suggests an alternate treatment by permitting or removing a portion of some food, we have achieved the best results.

Preceding getting into the cooking and changing your way of life from the very center with the goal of improving your health, we need you to become acquainted with renal eating routine fundamentals and discover precisely what his eating routine is based on, while you definitely understand what is the very center arrangement found in the renal eating regimen assisting you in improving your kidney's health by reducing sodium and potassium intake.

The most effective method of becoming acquainted with the renal eating routine and the essentials of this dietary routine is to investigate the most frequently asked inquiries that require a lengthy response. The renal diet is defined as follows:

When following a renal diet lifestyle, it is important to understand the components and what they do.

Considering that these are the most frequently asked questions, they should be able to answer a great deal of your questions about what a renal diet is and what it is not about.

Which foods should be avoided when following a renal diet?

Nutrition classes that may be harmful to an overall harmed renal framework and kidneys are restricted in the renal eating regimen, which is a dietary regimen. The primary goal of the eating regimen is to enable patients who have already been diagnosed with a type of kidney disease to maintain a better quality of life by enabling them to physically control the presence of sodium, potassium, water, and waste that should be generally controlled by healthy kidneys and normal renal capacity to continue living a healthy lifestyle. The provision of food varieties that are low in sodium and potassium is critical to the success of the renal eating regimen.

In order to perform my normal functions, how much protein do I require?

Protein requirements and requirements may differ from patient to patient, but in general, meat parts should be reduced to a bare minimum, and you should look for other sources of protein in alternative food choices other than meat items such as hamburger and chicken. The kidneys are in charge of protein digestion, and because you are dissatisfied with your renal capacities, you are keen to reduce your protein intake. All things considered, protein utilization should be maintained at a satisfactory level so that your body has the option to function properly. If you are not a dialysis patient, your normal protein intake should be somewhere in the range of 0.8 grams of protein per kilogram of your body weight every day. If you are a dialysis patient, your daily protein intake should be between 1 and 1.3 grams of protein per kilogram of your body weight. A solid weight-loss program that includes both physical activity and a healthy eating regimen is recommended if you are carrying around more weight than you should be carrying.

In a sense, protein assists our bodies in their recuperation, as the presence of a protein in our blood called egg whites manages both the development and the repair of harmed tissue, which is why protein is important.

When looking for protein sources, can I use meat substitutes?

In Relation to Kidney Disease, What Is Phosphorus?

Renal eating regimen encourages careful monitoring of potassium and sodium levels in your body, because, while these minerals are necessary for your body to function properly, excessive levels of these minerals can cause more medical issues and cause more harm to your kidneys than you might realize. In the same way, phosphorus levels in your body are affected by your lifestyle choices.

As a fundamental mineral that effectively maintains bone design while also dealing with the advancement of bone cells, phosphorus is addressed. Phosphorus is a fundamental mineral that plays an increasingly important role in our lives, chipping away at connective tissue repair and assisting in muscle development among other things. To be sure, when phosphorus concentrations are excessively high in your creature because your kidneys are unable to balance out phosphorus levels due to slow and impaired renal capacities, repetitive phosphorus becomes hazardous and may cause additional unexpected problems as well as aid in the progression of your persistent kidney's illness.. When phosphorus levels in your blood exceed recommended levels, the once-beneficial mineral turns into a danger to your health because phosphorus draws calcium from your bones, weakening them. Common signs and symptoms that appear as side effects in kidney patients who have elevated levels of phosphorus in their blood include heart calcification, weak and effectively brittle bones, muscle torment, as well as calcification of the skin and joints, as well as vein calcification. Due to the high levels of phosphorus in your blood that your damaged kidneys are unable to remove, calcium builds up and can affect your lungs, eyes, heart, and veins, causing further damage to your renal capacities that have already been compromised. For this reason, monitoring your phosphorus levels, in addition to monitoring your potassium and sodium levels, is critical for your renal health. This can be accomplished easily through the use of a suitable diet, such as the renal diet, which originally prescribed a low-sodium and low-potassium daily intake. As is the case with potassium and sodium, phosphorus is a mineral that can be found in a wide variety of food types, which means that intake of this essential mineral can be observed through food consumption.

A Guide to Lowering Phosphorus Levels Through a Renal Diet (Phosphorus in Food)

In the same way that you might limit your intake of potassium and sodium by avoiding foods that contain high concentrations of these minerals, you can also try to acquaint your body with healthy levels of phosphorus by following a healthy eating regimen. The entire way of thinking about lowering phosphorus levels, which should be controlled by your kidneys, is to reduce the intake of food sources that are high in this mineral in your diet. We do not recommend that you completely abandon phosphorus-rich nutrition classes because your body requires phosphorus regardless of how well your kidneys are doing. You should discuss this with your primary care physician to find out more about your phosphorus levels in your blood so that you can determine which foods you may have to give up on. You may want to keep an eye out for foods that contain high concentrations of phosphorus such as meat, cheddar, dairy, seeds, pop, seeds, and fast food varieties. You may also want to limit your overall consumption of protein and dairy, just as you would with foods that contain high concentrations of sodium and potassium. If your phosphorus levels are found to be higher than those recommended by your doctor, you will almost certainly be advised to reduce your consumption of meat and dairy products, as meat contains high concentrations of potassium as well.

It is best to restrict the nutrition classes that contain high concentrations of phosphorus, potassium, and sodium in your daily diet if you want to keep track of the amounts of these minerals you are absorbing. In addition to restricting food sources that contain undeniable levels of these minerals, you can also restrict the amount of phosphorus that is introduced into your organic entity by cutting out segments that contain foods that are high in phosphorus, potassium, or sodium. Try to figure out which nutritional categories contain the most noteworthy concentrations of phosphorus, and eating more fresh vegetables and natural products may be beneficial if you have a high level of phosphorus in your system. In general, foods that contain more than 120 mg of phosphorus per serving are considered to be high-phosphorus foods, and they should be introduced to your eating regimen slowly and gradually in smaller portions, just as is the case with foods that contain high amounts of potassium and sodium.

# Chapter Two

# What to Eat and What Not to Eat When It Comes to Phosphorus

We have included one more essential rundown to assist you with circling back to nutrition classes that are high in phosphorus as well as food varieties that have low concentrations of phosphorus. This list should assist you with your shopping on the off chance that you are attempting to bring down the amount of phosphorus introduced into your body by way of your food consumption.

Foods that are low in phosphorus (less than 120 mg per serving)

Cauliflower (baby)

Apple\sFigs

Cherries

berry natural products such as strawberry and blueberry Celery Fruit juice - organic Berry natural products such as celery and fruit juice

Radishes

Pears

Cabbage

Cucumber

The snow peas are a type of pea that grows in cold weather.

Cauliflower

Lettuce

Turnips

Even though you may need to keep an eye out for vegetables that are high in potassium, the majority of new veggies are low in phosphorus.

Cream cheddar and blue cheddar, for example, are two types of cheese. Make certain that your cheddar selections that are low in phosphorus are not at the same time high in potassium and sodium.

grain with pearls (pearlized barley)

Couscous

The color white is associated with pasta and rice.

# WHAT TO EAT AND WHAT NOT TO EAT WHEN IT COMES TO...

Bakery products made of white flour

The consumption of foods containing high levels of phosphorus.

Granules with a dark color

Grass that has not been refined.

Whole grains are a type of grain that contains all of the nutrients found in grains.

There are many different types of beans.

Vegetables that have been dehydrated

Dry fruits are a type of fruit that is dried and stored in a container.

Chocolate

Poultry\sBeef

Fish of various kinds have phosphorus fixations greater than 120 mg/kg of body weight

Phosphorus and potassium concentrations in meat are particularly high.

A high level of phosphorus is found in the majority of cheeses.

Make it a point to discuss a more customized diet with your primary care physician, and remember to take phosphate folios with each meal if your doctor suggests it. Patient's with impaired kidney function are frequently advised to take phosphate fasteners, as they are expected to ingest excessive amounts of the phosphate that has been introduced to the body through ingestion. If you are taking phosphate covers, consult with your doctor about which nutrition types from the list below you should eliminate, increase, or decrease in your intake.

# Chapter Three

# Renal Diets Should Contain Protein

Although it may appear, based on the recommendations in the book regarding protein intake, that renal eating regimen and protein do not mix well, this is neither an accurate nor a true statement. Renal eating regimen promotes healthy living in patients with low and impaired renal capacity, as well as in patients who are experiencing various stages of chronic kidneys infection. Its ultimate goal is to assist with improving renal wellbeing in patients who have been diagnosed with kidney disease, as well as in assisting with the prevention of ongoing kidney disease in patients who are at high risk of developing kidney disease in the future. When it comes to our bodies, protein is an essential nutrient that is required for a variety of vital functions, among which is the general ability to repair tissue and mend twisted wounds, as well as "maintaining" our overall weight. Patients may require additional protein, particularly if they have a portion of their body capacities that are frail, in order to be able to recover and work on their health. However, because the kidneys are responsible for protein metabolism,

Patients with damaged kidneys may experience "extras," which is an excessive amount of protein in their diet. The body becomes overloaded with harmful material because the kidneys are unable to eliminate all of the waste produced by the body's remaining organs while handling protein. That is the primary reason why renal diets advocate and recommend lower protein intakes for renal patients and individuals who are at high risk of developing an ongoing kidney infection. It goes without saying that there is no connection between the renal eating regimen and protein, as this eating regimen actually prescribes that you do not avoid protein dinners even if you do not consume meat. It is particularly recommended that protein be administered to renal patients after a successful kidney transplantation procedure, as they are in the recovery phase, during which protein is of critical importance. Based on the results of your experiments, consult with your primary care physician to determine how much protein you are permitted to consume on a consistent basis in order to meet more specific dietary needs.

Proteoproteins that are good for the kidneys

As previously stated, renal eating regimen DOES recommend lower protein dosages and more modest portions of meat for patients with ongoing kidney disease, but it DOES NOT recommend a complete lack of protein in your daily diet. There are numerous protein sources other than meat that can be described as tolerably cordial or completely renal eating regimen friendly and in accordance with dietary requirements, despite the fact that it is critical to consume your daily serving of protein. As previously stated in the book, the recommended portion of protein for renal patients is set at 0.8 mg of protein per kilogram of body weight and around 1.3 mg of protein per kilogram of body weight, unless otherwise recommended by your doctor.

A protein called egg whites was also mentioned, which is normally found in our blood and is responsible for the task of repairing tissue and maintaining tissue development. This is the reason you should not skip out on including protein to your eating regimen even if you are trying to eliminate meat segments from your eating regimen completely. In order to maintain healthy levels of egg whites and prevent further damage to your kidneys, we recommend a few top renal-friendly food options that will assist you in getting your daily protein requirement without jeopardizing your health or well-being.

Chicken

When your renal capacities are not performing optimally, chicken may contain an excess of potassium that you do not require, which is why it is recommended to reduce your protein intake. Regardless, lean chicken meat, particularly chicken bosoms, is particularly high in protein and low in fat, which is essentially what you want in a protein source, especially for vegetarians. Make an effort not to consume anything that contains chicken in it, such as pre-made chicken meal found in stores or handled and canned meat, which are high in potassium and sodium and should be avoided if you want to lose weight. As much as 28 grams of protein can be found in a single ounce of chicken meat.

Cheese

In spite of the fact that cottage cheddar may contain the ideal proportion of animal-based protein for your body, curds may contain higher concentrations of sodium despite the fact that it also contains unquestionable amounts of potassium. When looking for additional protein sources other than meat, experiment with low-sodium cheddar cheese. You should also keep in mind that low-sodium foods, such as cheddar, which have lower levels of this mineral, may contain higher levels of potassium, which you should avoid unless specifically advised otherwise by your doctor.

Eggs

You can eat egg substitutes that are low in sodium and potassium concentrations, but you can also eat eggs as long as you don't overdo it on the number of servings you consume. Egg whites, which contain approximately 7 grams of protein, are the most nutritious source of clean protein for you.

Yogurt

Try Greek yogurt instead of meat when substituting meat, assuming all else is equal, because this dairy product has fewer negative effects on your renal framework when compared to the negative effects that milk can have on your wellbeing while impairing your renal capacities. Approximately 20 grams of animal-based protein can be found in a single serving of Greek yogurt.

Burgers made from tofu

In situations where eating meat is not an option due to a specific reason, tofu burgers and other tofu items may be a good alternative source of protein, and a serving of tofu contains roughly the same amount of protein as the whites of one egg.

Shake for protein

Taking protein supplements that are in line with your renal eating regimen and recommended by your doctor may help. It is possible to incorporate protein enhancements into foods that have been grown from the ground, just as they can be added to your food, which can be a fantastic approach to adding protein in situations where there are no options for eating meat or obtaining protein from other sources.

Fish

Salmon, for example, contains up to 20 grams of protein per serving and, when compared to other fish, has lower potassium centralizations.

Keeping Protein in the Renal Diet under Control

The significance of cutting your protein segments when on a renal eating regimen, as well as figuring out how to consume enough protein so that you don't experience any additional health problems, has been emphasized in this article.

Because you should monitor your protein intake carefully so that you can devote your time to improving your overall health, we've put together a quick checklist of things you should pay particular attention to and keep an eye on.

Protein should be consumed in moderation so that it does not put additional strain on your vital organs. -

Checklist for Protein Control

Avoid handled meat, such as hotdogs, salami, canned meat, and other meat products that may contain higher concentrations of sodium and potassium than you are accustomed to.

Try to consume protein in the form of meat or fish only once per day to begin with. For your meat/fish meal, you could opt for lunch or dinner.

To make meat taste better, use less salt and instead season it with garlic powder, spices, and other safe flavors that we have listed in our Ultimate Renal Grocery List.

Instead of consuming charred meat, try baking, searing, barbecuing, or steam cooking your meat.

To improve your health, choose lean, fresh meat.

Portion control is key when it comes to protein intake.

## Choosing the Best Renal Food

In the same way that there are certain food categories that you should avoid consuming in order to maintain your renal health, there are certain food varieties that are considered "superfoods" when it comes to renal diet recommendations. Increasing your intake of these foods is encouraged because we selected the best renal food choices for people with low and damaged kidney capacities. We also explain why these foods are beneficial for both you and your kidney health.

## Blueberry

Considering that blueberry has remarkable cell-reinforcing properties, it follows that a combination of supplements found in this berry natural product should aid you in the management of harmful material, particularly in situations where your renal capacities are compromised.

The potassium and sodium concentrations in blueberry are low, and the phosphorus concentration is also low. Because of the combination of nutrients in this powerful organic product, the cell reinforcement bodies contained are capable of preventing a wide range of cardiovascular infections.

It is possible that red grapes in blueberry can aid in the prevention of cancerous growth, just as they can help you to avoid another high-potency natural product.

Potassium, phosphorus, and sodium are all concentrated in one place. Red grapes are a good source of L-ascorbic acid, which is beneficial for people who are on a renal diet because it provides a protected source of supplements. Furthermore, red grapes contain a specific type of cell reinforcement that has been demonstrated to be effective in reducing aggravation, which is yet another reason why red grapes should be incorporated into your everyday eating regimen. It is possible that this organic product will also aid in the prevention of diabetes and heart disease.

Garlic

As previously mentioned in the book, garlic is an excellent substitute for salt when it comes to lowering sodium levels in the body, which is also the case when following a renal diet. Using garlic as a salt substitute is a delicious way to add flavor to a dish while also benefiting from some of the amazing properties garlic possesses. As an excellent source of vitamin B6 and L-ascorbic acid, garlic has also been shown to have anti-inflammatory and anti-inflammatory properties, in addition to having a beneficial effect on the cardiovascular system. With potassium content, garlic is beneficial to the kidneys in particular.

## Cabbage

Cauliflower is one of the most remarkKable vegetables that you can incorporate into your regular eating regimen, assuming that the force of a vegetable is measured in terms of nutrients, minerals, and other essential nutrients. Beyond the fact that it contains low levels of potassium and other minerals that could be harmful to your damaged renal system, cabbage is a rich source of nutrients C and K, as well as vitamin B. So cabbage is a renal-accommodating food, but it also has a positive impact on your stomach-related wellbeing, providing fiber that great microscopic organisms can use for food, keeping your stomach-related wellbeing under wraps and free of contamination.

Bell Peppers are a type of pepper that is used to make a spicy sauce.

Chilli peppers are another excellent source of L-ascorbic acid, with a single large portion of the pepper providing sufficient amounts of the nutrient to meet your daily requirements. It also contains high concentrations of vitamin A, which has an impact on your immune system. In addition, it is loaded with significant amounts of cancer prevention agents, which have an impact on your immune system. It also contains low levels of sodium, phosphorus, and other agents. When it comes to renal diet, chili peppers are extremely beneficial.

potassium and sodium convergences are low in this case. Egg Whites are a type of white protein that can be found in large quantities in many dishes.

It is the protein in egg whites that gives your body the bulk it requires. Because your kidneys are having a difficult time dealing with the excess protein that quickly turns into harmful material, you are advised not to substitute animal-based protein; however, egg whites are recommended as a spotless source of unadulterated protein. For dialysis patients and patients who have already undergone a successful kidney transplant and are in need of high-quality protein sources, eggs are particularly recommended. Likewise, egg yolks are extremely nutritious and high in protein; however, because they contain high levels of phosphorus, they should not be consumed in large quantities. However, egg whites contain low concentrations of potassium, sodium, and phosphorus, making them one of the most kidney-friendly foods available today.

## Cauliflower

The use of cauliflower as a substitute for vegetables that are high in potassium, such as potatoes, will almost certainly become a favorite of yours. You can also use cauliflower as a substitute for rice that has lower levels of sugar if you are trying to reduce your carb intake. Due to the fact that cauliflower is low in potassium and sodium, and is also a poor source of phosphorus, this vegetable is an excellent source of vitamins and minerals for you to consume. Cauliflower is also a good source of vitamin K, A, and L-ascorbic acid, as well as a good source of fiber with anti-inflammatory properties, making it an excellent choice for people who need to adhere to a renal diet plan.

## Cranberries

People who suffer from ailments of the renal framework and kidneys, as well as those who simply dislike the feeling of having to go to the bathroom, will undoubtedly benefit from cranberry consumption. A special supplement verdure found in cranberries prevents various types of microbes from settling in the urinary tract, thereby reducing the risk of developing urinary tract diseases.

Cranberry is also kidney-friendly due to its exceptionally low potassium, phosphorus, and sodium concentrations, making it a safe source of nutrients for those following a renal diet. Even though you can consume fresh or cooked cranberries, such as cranberry sauce or freshly squeezed juice, it is recommended that you avoid eating dried natural products, including dried cranberries, while on the renal eating regimen.

## Onion

With its high fiber content, onions provide exceptional nourishment for your gastrointestinal microorganisms, allowing your stomach to remain healthy and well-protected by the beneficial microbes. Other than helping your stomach function properly and maintaining a healthy population of good bacteria, onions are low in potassium and sodium concentrations, as well as phosphorus concentrations, among other nutrients. Incorporate this nutrient-dense vegetable into your long-term dinner plans, while sautéed onions with garlic and a few tablespoons of olive oil are recommended for preparing your meat and preparing your dinners. A delicious substitute for salt, this blend contains significantly less sodium than salt and is therefore a healthier option for you. The presence of high concentrations of L- ascorbic acid and several types of vitamin B in onion makes it a fantastic source of supplements for your own health as well as your kidney's wellbeing.

## Pineapple

If you enjoy desserts and confections, pineapple may become your sweet getaway; however, pineapple is a far better choice than sweet treats if you are a fan of fruity treats. There are low concentrations of the elements phosphorus, potassium, and sodium in this sweet and appetizing natural product, which also has access to an abundant source of fiber and catalysts that have mitigating properties. One more reason to include this wonderful tropical organic product in your diet is that it is high in a variety of B vitamins, which are essential for good health. Breasts of chicken

Chicken breasts are a lean meat that is high in protein, and they are probably the best choice for your animal-based protein as long as you buy chicken breasts that do not have skin on them and as long as you manage to keep your meat portions small and moderately added to your daily diet as recommended. The potassium, sodium, and phosphorus levels in chicken bosoms are higher than those found in virtually any other type of meat; however, skinless chicken bosoms prepared slowly cooked or heated for specific vegetables can be a fantastic source of protein for people following a renal diet. Skin the chicken before cooking it, and season with garlic and other low-sodium ingredients other than salt to make it more flavorful and nutritious.

Mushrooms (Shiitake)

Mushrooms can be used as an alternative protein source in the case of a vegetarian or vegan diet, or in the event that you are avoiding meat altogether. When compared to other types of mushrooms, shiitake mushrooms are particularly beneficial to include in your diet because they contain lower levels of potassium than the others. Beyond providing significant amounts of protein and a relatively low amount of potassium, shiitake mushrooms are also high in selenium, copper, and B vitamins, while also containing relatively little sodium and a high concentration of copper.

Arugula

It is another low-potassium vegetable that can serve as an excellent substitute for greens such as kale and spinach, which contain higher amounts of potassium, while also serving as an excellent source of vitamin K. Arugula is also a good source of fiber. As an added benefit, arugula contains high levels of nitrates, which help to lower blood pressure, which is important for kidney health because high blood pressure can cause more damage to your kidneys while also serving as one of the primary indicators that something is wrong with your kidneys because of elevated sodium levels and other risk factors. We encourage you to include arugula as a side dish or in your mixed greens salads as a source of calcium in addition to the other vegetables.

The following are some strategies/tips on how to behave during an interstitial kidney diet.

It is necessary to follow a renal diet if you suffer from kidney disappointment, a harmed kidney, or the side effects of kidney issues. The renal eating regimen focuses in particular on the food sources that should be avoided because they are inconvenient to the health of your kidneys.

This eating regimen regulates your body's utilization of sodium, protein (including casein), potassium, and phosphorus.. In addition to preventing renal disappointment, a renal eating regimen can be beneficial. The following is a list of foods and supplements that you should consume to avoid kidney-related problems: Phosphate: When kidney disappointment reaches 80 percent and the patient is in the fourth or fifth phase of kidney disappointment, the consumption of phosphate becomes dangerous. In this vein, it is preferable to reduce your phosphate intake by counting calories and minerals. For those following a renal eating regimen, you should allow 0.75 kg of protein per day as a guideline. Eggs, milk, cheddar, meat, nuts, and fish are excellent sources of protein.

Potassium: If your potassium level in the blood is found to be excessive after being tested, you should reduce your potassium intake. Potassium levels in potatoes, both prepared and smoked, are very high. High in potassium are salad greens and organic fruit juices.

Vegetables that are low in potassium can be appreciated in any case.

Amount of sodium in our food is essential, but if you have kidney problems, you should avoid or limit your salt intake to prevent further damage. Overabundance of sodium intake can result in hypertension and increased liquid retention in the body. Find substitutes that will assist you in the preparation of your food if possible. Extracted from plants flavors and spices make for an acceptable substitute. You can enhance the flavor of your food without adding salt if you use garlic, pepper, and mustard in your preparations.

Maintain a healthy sodium intake while avoiding low sodium counterfeit "salts" that are high in potassium, which is harmful to kidney health as well.

# Chapter Four

# THE RECIPES

Cooking Ideas for the Morning

omelette with egg whites and peppers

METHOD OF DESCRIPTION: COOKING TIME: 5 MIN

Red ringer peppers are used in this low-calorie omelet recipe, which can be prepared in less than 5 minutes with just five ingredients. Paprika or Mexican spices may be used to enhance the flavor of your dish.

Ingredients for 1-2 servings (about).

Soft beaten egg whites (four)

1 red chile pepper, peeled and chopped

1 tsp. of paprika (optional).

olive oil (around 2 tablespoons)

12-tablespoon (or equivalent amount) of salt

Pepper

Heat the olive oil in a shallow dish (about 8 inches) and sauté the mushrooms.

Peppers are softened with ringer sauce.

Overlapping the edges into the liquid area with a spatula will help to cook your omelet until the eggs are entirely opaque and firm, which will take around 15 minutes.

Sea salt and freshly ground pepper are used for seasoning.

3 people are needed to complete this task.

THE NUTRITIONAL INFORMATION FOR EACH SERVING (IN CALORIES):

Grain sugar (3.8 g):

9.2g of protein

797 milligrams of sodium

Potassium is 193 milligrams.

202.5 milligrams of phosphorus

1. Dietary fiber is 0.75 grams per day

15.22 g of dietary fat

Stage 2 of renal disease

Smoothie bowl with blueberries

frozen blueberries (about 12 cup total)

12 cup almond milk with a vanilla flavoring sugar substitute (such as agave syrup) 1 tablespoon

cup of chia seeds (about 1 tablespoon)

METHOD

Then mix everything but the chia seeds until it's silky smooth, around 30 seconds. You should be left with a thick smoothie as a result of your efforts.

paste.

Fill an oat bowl halfway with the mixture and sprinkle with chia seeds.

Calories: 278.5 kcal per serving; Nutritional Information (per serving)

387.72 grams of carbohydrates

1.3g of protein

the amount of sodium in 76.33 milliliters

229,1 milligrams of potassium

592 milligrams (mg) of phosphorus

7.4 grams of dietary fiber

6 g of lipids

## THE FIRST STAGE OF KIDNEY DISEASE

Breakfast Sausage made with turkey.

## 6 MINUTES FOR PREP AND COOK DESCRIPTION

For breakfast or an early lunch, a quick hotdog will suffice. Make this low-potassium breakfast wiener with turkey and flavors to see how it works. Serve this with cornbread and apple sauce if you want to be really fancy.

## FOR 12 SERVINGS, USE THESE INGREDIENTS

Each recipe makes 12 patties.

1 pound of ground turkey that has been trimmed of excess fat.

Fennel seed (1 teaspoon) and garlic powder (1/4 teaspoon) are used in this recipe.

onion powder (14 tbsp.)

salt (14 tbsp.

Vegetable oil (about 2 tbsp.)

Pepper

All of the ingredients, save the vegetable oil, should be mixed together.

mix it all together in a blender

Create long, level patties (about 4 inches long). 3. In a medium-sized broiling pan, heat the vegetable oil until shimmering.

Cook for about 3 minutes on each side after adding 3-4 patties at a time to the pan.

side. Cook the patties one at a time until they are all done.

Warm up the dish before serving it to guests.

INFORMATION ON NUTRITIONAL PRODUCTS (Per Serving)

74 kilocalories (calories)

Glycemic Index (GI): 0.1 g

7 grams of protein

120.91 milligrams of sodium

The following is the amount of potassium in grams: 89.5 mg

Calcium: 75 milligrams

Fibre from plant sources: zero grams

5.16 g of lipids

METHOD FOR DIAGNOSTIC OF KIDNEY DISEASE STAGE 2

4. Apple Fritters in the Italian Style.

8 MINUTES FOR COOKING DESCRIPTION A quick glazed doughnut recipe that uses corn flour as a star ingredient that

is fantastic for breakfast and pastries. Make this in a deep fryer and eat it immediately since it will lose its freshness within a number of minutes if not served immediately after preparation. COMPOSITION FOR FOUR SERVINGS

spherical circles of thickly cut apples that have been seeded, peeled, and thickly sliced

1 cup cornmeal, 3 tablespoons oil

Water (about 12 teaspoons)

Sugar (1 teaspoon)

Cinnamon, 1 teaspoon (or more)

Oil derived from plants (for frying)

sugar or honey strewn on the surface

Combine the corn flour, water, and sugar in a small mixing basin to form your batter.

Into the cornflour mixture, the apple is assimilated.

Using a medium to high heat, heat enough vegetable oil to coat half the surface of the container.

Toss in the apple slices and heat until they are a bright golden color.

Sprinkle a little cinnamon and icing sugar over the top of the mixture in a shallow dish with retaining paper on top.

INFORMATION ON NUTRITIONAL PRODUCTS (Per Serving)

183 kcal (calories)

17.9 g of carbohydrates

0.3g of protein

2 g of sodium

One hundred milligrams (100mg) of potassium

1.25 gram of phosphorus

1.4 grams of dietary fiber

14.17 g of fat

METHOD FOR DIAGNOSTIC OF KIDS WITH KIDS WITH KIDS WITH KIDS

13th, Mushroom Rice Noodles.

This recipe makes four servings of each ingredient.

TIME FOR PREP AND COOK: 15 MINUTES TIME FOR FINISHING: 15 MINUTES

THERE IS LITTLE PROTEIN AND FAT IN THIS FOOD Some of the best Asian cuisines, such as pad Thai and pho, begin with rice noodles, which are available in a variety of shapes and sizes. When looking for the Asian noodles for this meal, you'll find yourself presented with packets of many varieties, including udon, soba, and lo mein. Look for basic rice noodles that are uncomplicated and around 14 inches in width or wider. Because they include additional ingredients such as buckwheat, the nutritional information may alter depending on the kind you choose..

Noodles made with 4 cups of rice

2 teaspoons of sesame oil that has been lightly roasted. wild mushrooms (about 2 cups) sliced garlic, minced (about 2 tablespoons)

1-inch-thick red bell pepper, cut 1-inch-thick yellow bell pepper, sliced

1 tablespoon of low-sodium soy sauce, sliced scallions (white and green sections)

METHOD

Rice noodles should be prepared according to the package guidelines and then put aside.

Preparing the sesame oil begins by heating it in a large pan over medium high heat. 3. Sauté the red ringer pepper, yellow chime pepper, carrot, and scallions until they are soft and translucent, about 5 minutes total time.

In a separate bowl, combine the soy sauce and rice noodles and mix well. 5. Put it on the table and eat it!

Sodium-reduced recommendation Because it contains roughly 360 mg of sodium per tablespoon, liquid aminos (also known as coconut aminos)-a sauce that has mostly been retired beside the soy sauce in general stores-is an acceptable alternative for soy sauce. When it comes to salt, regular soy sauce has around 920 mg per tablespoon, while low-sodium soy sauce contains approximately 575 mg per tablespoon.

## HEALTHY EATING DIRECTIONS

The following are the calories per serving: 163 per serving

2 grams of total fat Glycemic index: 0 g Zero milligrams of cholesterol Amount of sodium: 199 milligrams 33.3 g of carbohydrate 2 grams of fiber 69 milligrams of phosphorus. The following is the potassium content: 200 mg 2 grams of protein

4th Stage of Kidney Failure

Vegetable Barley with a Variety of Vegetables 14

## INGREDIENTS

Olive oil, 1 tablespoon (about)

finely sliced medium-sweet onion cup of fresh cauliflower florets, 2 tablespoons minced garlic, and 2 teaspoons oil red pepper, diced (one red bell pepper)

1-cup chopped carrots

12 cup of barley is used in this recipe.

12 cup of white rice (or other grain of choice). Water (around 2 glasses)

Fresh parsley, finely minced (about 1 tablespoon)

SERVES 6 PEOPLE WITH THIS METHOD

TIME ALLOWED FOR PREP: 15 MIN TIME TO PREPARE: 35 MINUTES TIME TO COOK

THERE IS LITTLE PROTEIN AND FAT IN THIS FOOD Barley is a cereal grain that is often included in soups because it provides solidity, thickens the stock a little, and has a pleasing chewy surface to it. With high levels of manganese, molybdenum, and fiber, grain is an excellent choice for regulating the stomach associated structure and lowering cholesterol, as well as lowering the risk of cardiovascular disease and other chronic conditions. When making this dish, either pearl grain or pot grain will provide the greatest results.

The olive oil should be heated in a large pan over medium-high heat.

In a large skillet, heat the oil over medium heat until it is warm, about 3 minutes.

Sauté for 5 minutes after adding the cauliflower, ringer pepper, and carrots.

Bring the grain, rice, and water to a boil in a large pot, stirring often.

Reduce the heat to low, cover, and simmer for about 25 minutes, or until the liquid has been retained and the grain and rice are soft.

Garnish with parsley at the end of the meal.

Culinary Tip: You may make this meal under the broiler rather than in the oven, and you can prepare it completely the night before. Simply transfer the sautéed veggies to an 8-by-8-inch baking dish and stir in the grain, rice, and water until everything is evenly distributed. Refrigerate until you are ready to bake with it.

CALORIES IN EACH SERVING PER SERVING NUTRITIONAL INFORMATION

3 grams of total fat

Glycemic index: 0 g

Zero milligrams of cholesterol

16.4 milligrams of sodium

Approximately 30 g of carbohydrate.

4 grams of fiber 83 milligrams of phosphorus.

The following is the potassium content: 210 mg 4 grams of protein

Stage 5 of kidney disease

Sesame Tofu with a Spicy Kick

15 MINUTES PREP TIME COOK TIME: 10 MINUTES SERVES 6
PREP TIME COOK TIME

THERE IS LITTLE PROTEIN AND FAT IN THIS FOOD Because they have no idea how to put up these squares of squeezed soy, even the most devoted vegetarians sometimes pass right by the tofu exhibit at the supermarket. The same way that cheddar is manufactured, tofu may be purchased in a variety of textures ranging from delicate to very hard, depending on how much liquid has been squeezed out of it. Incredibly versatile, tofu is a fantastic mending.

## INGREDIENTS

Toasted sesame oil absorbs any tastes that are added to it and may be used to create concoctions that are both fresh and solid. The

In this recipe, the flavors of sesame, ginger, soy sauce, and hot red pepper bits combine to create a really amazing mixture for imbuing the tofu with flavor and nutrients.

fresh ginger, grated and peeled (about a tablespoon) minced garlic, 2 tablespoons

thinly sliced red bell peppers (red peppers)

Extra-firm tofu (14-ounce container), drained and sliced into 1-inch chunks.

cups of bok choy, quartered

Salad scallions, white and green portions, finely sliced and on the bias

teaspoon soy sauce with reduced sodium

Lime juice (freshly squeezed): 2 teaspoons Red pepper flakes (around a pinch)

cilantro, 2 teaspoons finely chopped Sesame seeds, 2 teaspoons, roasted

METHOD

Sesame oil should be heated in a large pan over medium-high heat. Cook for about 3 minutes, or until the ginger and garlic have softened. After you've added the ringer peppers and tofu, softly cook it for roughly three minutes on medium heat. ***

Toss in the broccoli and scallions and cook, stirring often, for 3 minutes, or until the broccoli is shrivelled. Using your hands, cover the red pepper chunks with soy sauce, lime juice, and other seasoning.

Garnish with cilantro and sesame seeds at the end of the serving.

Advice on eating low in sodium: Because soy sauce accounts for almost all of the sodium in this meal, reducing or eliminating it will result in a significant reduction in the sodium content of each serving of the dish. The taste of the formula will not be as strong, but using just 1 tablespoon of soy sauce in this formula will result in a presentation that has around 160 mg of salt.

EACH SERVING CONTAINS NUTRITIONAL DATA. Approximately 80 calories. 3 grams of total fat

Glycemic index: 0 g Zero milligrams of cholesterol 503 milligrams of sodium 4 grams of carbohydrates 1 gram of dietary fiber. 88 milligrams of phosphorus. K is 165 milligrams (mg). 6 grams of protein

Stage 5 of kidney disease

Recipes for Lunch

Sauce de Cochinita Creame with Cidre

25 MINUTES FOR COOKING

DESCRIPTION OF THE MINUTES

In less than 30 minutes, you may have a delicious meal made using a simple 4-fixing method. This meal is fantastic for a mid-week family supper or even as a welcome dish for guests! For that extra kick of taste, a mild sauce has been added.

COMPOSITION FOR 8 SERVINGS: INGREDIENTS:

1 pound chicken breasts with the skin on

light salted butter, 2 tablespoons

34-cup of apple cider vinegar is a good amount.

3 cups unsweetened coconut milk or cream, preferably unsweetened Kosher

pepper

METHOD

Using a skillet, melt the margarine over a medium heat.

The pepper should be sprinkled over the chicken before placing it in the pan. Allow about 20 minutes of cooking time on a low heat.

Take the chicken out of the hotness and place it in a plate to keep it cool.

Cook until the liquid has almost completely evaporated in a similar pan, until the juice has almost completely evaporated.

Cook for 1 minute, or until the coconut cream is just thickened, before adding more.

Serve the chicken with the juice cream over it once it has cooked.

INFORMATION ON NUTRITIONAL PRODUCTS (Per Serving)

Nutritional Values: 86.76 kcals

1.88 grams of carbohydrates

1.5g of protein

It contains 93.52 milligrams of sodium.

the following amount of potassium: 74.65 milligrams

36.544mg of phosphorus

The following is the nutritional fiber content: 0.1g

8.21 g of lipids

End-Stage Renal Disease

17) Macaroni and Cheese, which is simple and quick to make

8-10 MINUTES FOR THE COOKING DESCRIPTION Among both children and adults, mac-and-cheese is the most popular southern dish. It's

As it stands, it is not what we would call "solid."

Even though it is high in carbohydrates, it is acceptable when following a renal diet because it is extremely low in potassium and phosphorus.

COMPOSITION FOR FOUR SERVINGS

elbow macaroni (dried) 1 cup (serves 4)

mild cheddar cheese (approximately 12 cups) Water (three cups)

Unsalted butter (one tablespoon)

Dry mustard powder (approximately 12 teaspoon)

TWO TABLESPOONS OF PIMENTO CHEESE

In a large pot of boiling water, cook the elbow macaroni for 7-8 minutes (or until soft).

Make sure you drain all of your water before putting your bowl in the sink!

While the pasta is still hot, toss in the spread cheddar, mustard, and paprika and toss again.

INFORMATION ON NUTRITIONAL PRODUCTS (Per Serving)

The calories in this recipe are 231.68 kcal each. Carbohydrates: 32.65 grams

9.74g of protein Sodium:\s107.25mg K - 29.52 milligrams Potassium 159.93 mg of phosphorus The amount of dietary fiber is 0.12 grams. 7.2g of fat

2nd stage of kidney disease

Palbok, a rare and endangered species

12-15 MINUTES FOR THE COOKING DESCRIPTION It is a delicious Filipino recipe that combines different types of rice noodles and shrimp together.

PACKAGE CONTAINS ENOUGH FOOD FOR SIX SERVINGS

Approximately 12 ounces of rice noodles 1

3 spring onions, thinly sliced 12 cups medium shrimp, peeled and deveined 2 3 cup white onion, chopped 1 spring onion, thinly sliced

lean ground turkey, pound for pound

firm tofu, diced (about 2 cups).

shrimp or regular gravy mix (up to 2 packages). 5

lemon 1 lemon juice 2 hard-boiled eggs

pork rinds (about 12 cup) (optional)

## METHOD

Rice noodles should be cooked until they are very soft and flexible. Remove from the picture and put it somewhere safe.

Using plain water, bring the stripped shrimp to a boil for 2-3 minutes.

Sauté the garlic and onion in the oil in a wok or shallow skillet until soft. Prepare your ingredients by combining the ground turkey, tofu, and shrimps in a large mixing bowl.

Sauce blend should be dispersed in water (or other liquid) according to the package directions.

Using 12 cup of pork skin, mix together the rice noodles, tofu, onions, and sauce blend (optional).

Chop the lemon and egg slices into thin slices. (Optional)

1. Serve with a fried egg and slices of lemon on top. 2.

## INFORMATION ON NUTRITIONAL PRODUCTS (Per Serving)

305 kcal of energy

The following is the amount of carbohydrates: 39.14g

17.6g of rotein

536mg of enmity.

243.52 mg of potassium

the amount of hosphorus in 180.41mg

ietary 0.9 g of fiber

Stage 4 of kidney disease METHOD

Curry with Gobi (Vegetable)

## 15 MINUTES FOR THE COOKING DESCRIPTION

An ethnic Indian formula that originates in the Gobi Desert region, with a velvety and hot flavor and a surface that is a haven for people of all ages and backgrounds. Due to the fact that it is both delicious and filling, vegans will enjoy this formula.

## INGREDIENTS

2 cups of florets from a head of cauliflower. Unsalted butter, 2 tablespoons

medium white onion, thinly chopped (about 1 medium onion)

Green peas (about 12 cup) (frozen if wish) fresh ginger, finely chopped 1 tbsp. soy sauce

Turmeric (a teaspoonful)

Garam masala (about 1 tsp.

a quarter-teaspoon cayenne pepper

a tablespoon of liquid

Melt the margarine in a skillet over medium heat and cook the onions until they are caramelized (brilliant brown).

In a separate bowl, combine the spices, such as the ginger and garam masala. Pour the cauliflower and frozen peas into the pan and stir well to combine them. 4.

Cover the container with a lid to keep the water in. Reduce the heat to a low setting and allow the dish to cook for 10 minutes while still covered with foil.

White rice should accompany this dish.

INFORMATION ON NUTRITIONAL PRODUCTS (Per Serving)

91.04 kcal per serving Grain: 7.3g Carbohydrate 2.19 g of proteins 41,38 milligrams (mg) of sodium The following is the potassium content: 209.58 milligrams (mg). 42 milligrams of phosphorus Fibre from plant sources: 3 grams 6.4 gram of fat

2nd stage of kidney disease

20. Shrimp and Pasta with Marination

10 MINUTES FOR COOKING

DESCRIPTION OF THE MINUTES

Shrimps, pasta, and a variety of vegetables are combined in a generous formula for an explosion of tones and flavors in this dish. For lunch or as a visitor's dish, try this extraordinary pasta salad.

COMPLETE INGREDIENTS FOR 10 CUPS

12-ounce package of penne pasta in three different hues

Cooked shrimp weighing 12 pounds

diced one-half of a red bell pepper

Red onion, chopped to a 12 cup serving size

a few celery stalks

12 baby carrots, peeled and sliced thickly

cauliflower, cut into small round pieces (about 1 cup total).

Honey (about a quarter cup)

Balsamic vinegar (about 14 cup)

black pepper, 12 tsp. a.

garlic powder (approximately 12 teaspoon)

french mustard (about 1 tablespoon)

olive oil (about a third of a cup)

METHOD

Pasta should be cooked for approximately ten minutes (or as indicated by bundled instructions).

Prepare all of your vegetables and place them in a large mixing bowl while your pasta is cooking. Cooked shrimp should be added at this stage.

3. Place the honey, vinegar, dark pepper, garlic powder, and mustard in a blender and blend until smooth. 4. Slowly incorporate the oil while whisking continuously.

In a separate bowl, mix together the depleted pasta, vegetables, and shrimp, gently combining everything together. Mix in the pasta and vegetables with the marinade after it has been poured on top of them.

Allow for 3-5 hours in the refrigerator before serving. Allow to cool before serving.

INFORMATION ON NUTRITIONAL PRODUCTS (Per Serving)

256 kilocalories (calories)

Carbohydrates: 41 grams 6.55 g (of protein) 248.04 milligrams of sodium Amount of potassium in milligrams (mg) 86.03 mg of phosphorus 2.28 g of dietary fiber Fat:

16.88g

End-Stage Renal Disease

a sandwich made with steak and onions, number twenty-one.

## METHOD

### 8 MINUTES PREP AND COOK TIME DETAILS

When you want to eat something delicious but don't have a lot of time, this rich steak sandwich is a great option. This dish can be prepared ahead of time and served for lunch the following day, or it can be enjoyed fresh with the rest of your family.

### COMPOSITION FOR FOUR SERVINGS

4 fillets de Boeuf Bourguignon (around 4 oz. each) slices of one medium-sized red onion

1 tablespoon freshly squeezed lemon juice (optional).

seasoning (Italian seasoning, 1 tablespoon) black pepper (about 1 tsp.

vegetable oil (about 1 tbsp.) 4 buns for a sandwich or a hamburger

Using a lemon wedge, Italian seasoning, and pepper to taste, wrap the steak in a plastic wrap. Using four pieces, cut the cake. In a medium-sized skillet, heat the vegetable oil over medium heat until hot.

To achieve a medium to well-done result, cook the steaks for about 3 minutes per side. Removing the engrossing paper from the dish and placing it on a new dish

Continue to cook the onions until they are soft and straightforward in a separate skillet until they are done (around 3 minutes).

Using a sharp knife, cut the sandwich bun in half and place one piece of steak in each half, finishing with onions. Serve immediately or wrap in waxed paper or aluminum foil and store in the refrigerator for the day after. INFORMATION ON NUTRITIONAL PRODUCTS (Per Serving)

315.26 kcal (calories) 8.47 grams of carbohydrates 38.33g of protein 266.24 milligrams sodium The following is the potassium content: 238.2 milligrams The following is the phosphorus content: 364.425 mg The following amount of dietary fiber is consumed: 0.76 grams 13.22g of fat

2nd stage of kidney disease

# Chapter Five

# Crab Cakes with a Kick

## 6 MINUTES FOR THE COOKING DESCRIPTION

Children and adults alike enjoy crab cakes, which are a popular dish in American fish restaurants and are enjoyed by both children and adults. For those who enjoy crab cakes, try this delectable recipe that is completely free of liability because it is extremely low in phosphorus and potassium.

Ingredients for the METHOD SERVINGS FOR 6 PEOPLE

Crab meat weighing 9 ounces (250 grams).

15 tablespoons of green or red ringer pepper, finely chopped

Crushed wafers with low sodium content (13 cup)

14 cup low-fat mayonnaise (or other similar condiment).

mustard (dry): 1 tablespoon

salt and pepper to taste 12 tbsp.

lemon juice (about 2 tbsp.)

Lemon zest (approximately 12 teaspoons)

garlic powder (about a tablespoon)

Vegetable oil (about 2 tbsp.)

Except for the oil, combine all of the ingredients until they are uniform in color. Six level patties were created (around 5 creeps in diameter).

Deep-fry the patties for 2-3 minutes on each side in a skillet filled with vegetable oil after heating it up (or until brilliant brown).

Put it in a dish lined with retaining paper and serve it while it is still warm.

INFORMATION ON NUTRITIONAL PRODUCTS (Per Serving)

144.42 kcal per serving 5.12 grams of carbohydrates 8.47g of protein 212.31 milligrams of sodium the following amount of potassium: 195 milligrams the element phosphorus is 127.42mg. 1.02 g of dietary fiber 9.2 g of lipids

Stage 5 of kidney disease

Sautéing Tofu with Hoisin

15 MINUTES PREP TIME (20 MINUTES COOK TIME) SERVES 4 TIME TO PREPARE: 15 MINUTES

You'll be satisfied with the taste if you enjoy spicy, spicy food. This recipe makes use of an entire jalapeo pepper to create an intricate heat that isn't overly mouth-scorching.

Choose green peppers rather than red ones, and steer clear of peppers that have white striations running through them if you're looking for something mild.

INGREDIENTS

the hoisin sauce (about two tablespoons)

1 cup rice vinegar, 2 tablespoons tamari

1 teaspoon of cornstarch (or similar quantity).

2 tablespoons of extra-virgin olive oil poured down the sides of the pan lengthwise As the pepper grows older, the striations become more prominent, which corresponds to it becoming infinitely hotter.

Tofu, cut into 1-inch cubes, from a 15-ounce package of extra-firm tofu

Unpeeled, cubed eggplant (about 2 cups).

Slicing 2 scallions, both the white and green parts

garlic, minced (about 2 tablespoons)

2 tablespoons minced jalapeo pepper

chopped fresh cilantro, 2 tablespoons

METHOD

In a small mixing bowl, whisk together the hoisin sauce, rice vinegar, and cornstarch until well combined. Set this aside for later use.

The olive oil should be heated in a large pan over medium-high heat. Sauté the tofu until it is a brilliant brown color, about 10 minutes, then transfer to a serving dish to cool.

Medium heat should be used instead of high heat. Sauté the eggplant, scallions, garlic, and jalapeo pepper for about 6 minutes, or until the eggplant is soft and fragrant. Remove from the heat and set aside..

Cook, stirring constantly, for approximately 2 minutes, until the sauce thickens. Stir in the tofu and cilantro until well combined, then serve while still hot.

Sodium-reduced recommendation Because hoisin sauce is made with soy sauce, it contains a significant amount of sodium in each serving of the condiment. This recipe would still be delicious, albeit a little less strongly seasoned, if you used 1 tablespoon of hoisin sauce instead of 2 tablespoons.

EACH SERVING CONTAINS NUTRITIONAL DATA. Nutritional Values: 105 Calories

4 grams of total fat

1 gram of saturated fat.

Zero milligrams of cholesterol

234 milligrams of sodium

9 g of carbohydrate

2 grams of fiber

105 milligrams of phosphorus.

K is 192 milligrams (mg).

8 grams of protein

2nd stage of kidney disease

## 24. Curry with Sweet Potatoes

6 PEOPLE MAY BE SERVED

THE PREP AND COOK TIME WILL TAKE 20 MINUTES TO COMPLETE.

PROTEIN CONCENTRATION IS LOW. Sweet potatoes contain a moderate amount of potassium, but the amount is within acceptable limits when consumed in small quantities, such as in this curry recipe. Yams are a fantastic source of betacarotene, fiber, vitamin A, and lascorbic acid, and they are also high in potassium. Regardless of the fact that you are most likely accustomed to vibrant orange yams, don't be surprised if you cut into one and discover deep purple tissue within. Anthocyanins, found in purple yams, are powerful antioxidants that help the body fight disease.

INGREDIENTS

olive oil (two teaspoons)

1 medium sweet onion, peeled and finely minced

1/4 cup grated fresh ginger, peeled and chopped

1 teaspoon of finely minced garlic, fresh from the harvest

2 cups of diced sweet potatoes with the peels removed.

Carrots (about a cup) diced

Water (one cup)

heavy (whipping) cream (about 12 cup)

one-quarter teaspoon curry powder

ground cumin (about 1 teaspoon)

plain low-fat yogurt (about 2 tablespoons)

cilantro, freshly cleaved, 2 tablespoons

METHOD

The olive oil should be heated in a large pot over medium-high heat.

Continue to cook for about 3 minutes or until the onion, ginger, and garlic are soft and slightly browned.

Blend all of the ingredients together until smooth, including the yams, carrots, cream, curry powder, and cumin. Bring the mixture to a boil over medium-high heat. Heat to a gentle simmer for 15 minutes, or until the vegetables are tender and the sauce has thickened slightly.

Finish with the yogurt and cilantro and serve immediately.

Helpful hints on how to substitute Almost any vegetable will work in a dish like curry, so don't be afraid to let your creative juices run wild! If you want to make sure that your mineral levels are within the proper range, stick to the kidney-friendly vegetables listed in this book (see Phosphorus here and Potassium here).

EACH SERVING CONTAINS NUTRITIONAL DATA. Calories in a serving (132 calories).

9 grams of total fat

Total fat: 5 g saturated fat

The cholesterol level is 27 milligrams.

40% of the recommended daily allowance of Sodium

There are 13 grams of carbohydrates in this recipe.

2 grams of fiber

Calcium: 48 milligrams

The following is the potassium content: 200 mg

1 g of protein

Symptoms of Stage 1 Kidney Disease

## Spring Vegetables and Zucchini Noodles (#25)

6 PEOPLE MAY BE SERVED

20 minutes to prepare; 10 minutes to cook. Preparation time is 20 minutes; Cooking time is 10 minutes.

EXTREMELY LOW PROTEIN AND EXTREMELY LOW FAT On your plate, stores of vegetable noodles, asparagus lances, and full cherry tomatoes may appear as if they are freshly harvested and especially welcoming. Due to the fact that

INGREDIENTS

cut 6 zucchini into long spaghetti-like strands.

1 cup of divided snow peas vegetables, these noodles don't taste anything like pasta, but you can twist them around a fork and suck them up like spaghetti if you want to. Given a medium to large, firm zucchini and a spiralizer (see Cooking tip), you can turn out strands that are a few feet long, allowing you to decide whether to make them more or less restricted in size. (If you don't have a spiralizer, you can make the veggie noodles with a vegetable peeler instead.) In a sealed container, zucchini noodles can be stored in the refrigerator for up to 3 days.

one-cup of asparagus (cut into 3-inch chunks)

Olive oil, 1 tablespoon (about)

1 teaspoon of finely minced garlic, fresh from the harvest

lemon juice (freshly squeezed): 1 teaspoon

new spinach that has been ruined 1 cup

split cherry tomatoes (about a cup and a quarter)

freshly chopped basil leaves (about 2 tablespoons)

METHOD

To boil the water, fill a medium-sized pot halfway with water and set it over a medium-high heat.

Turn down the heat to medium, and blanch the zucchini strips, snow peas, and asparagus by lowering them into the boiling water for 1 second each. Submerge in a channel of cold water and flush thoroughly. Transfer the vegetables to a large mixing bowl after they have been thoroughly dried with paper toweling.

Warm up the olive oil in a medium-sized skillet over medium heat until it begins to shimmer. Add the garlic and cook for 3 minutes, or until it's soft and fragrant.

Add the lemon juice and spinach and cook, stirring frequently, for about 3 minutes, or until the spinach has shrivelled.

In a large mixing bowl, combine the zucchini mixture, cherry tomatoes, and basil until well combined.

Serve as soon as possible after preparing it.

Spiralizers are an excellent investment for the home chef. It is possible to create amazing long noodles from soil products using this reasonable culinary device, which can then be presented in a unique way.

EACH SERVING CONTAINS NUTRITIONAL DATA. Nutritional Values: 52 calories per serving

2 grams of total fat

Glycemic index: 0 g

Zero milligrams of cholesterol

7.4 milligrams of sodium

4 grams of carbohydrates

1 gram of dietary fiber.

40 milligrams of phosphorus

K is 197 milligrams (mg).

2 grams of protein

4th Stage of Kidney Failure

Recipes for Snack Food

# Chapter Six

# Apple Chips with Cinnamon

SERVES 4 • PREP TIME: 5 MINUTES 2 – 3 HOURS FOR THE COOKING

Chips, for example, have a certain addictive quality to them that makes you want to consume more of them. Nutrients, fiber, and delicious flavor are all provided by this righteous chip. Cilantro, a flavorful and warming zest, aids in digestion while also supporting the spleen, kidneys, and lungs, making it an excellent addition to your diet and these chips, as well as to any dish that includes it.

INGREDIENTS

4 apples are used in this calculation.

ground cinnamon (about 1 teaspoon)

METHOD

Preheat the broiler to 200°F. Line a baking sheet with parchment paper.

Core the apples and cut into ⅛-inch slices.

In a medium bowl, throw the apple cuts with the cinnamon. Spread the apples in a solitary layer on the pre-arranged baking sheet.

Cook for 2 to 3 hours, until the apples are dry. They will in any case be delicate while hot however will fresh once totally cooled. Store in a water/air proof holder for up to four days. Cooking tip: If you don't have material paper, use cooking splash to forestall sticking.

## HEALTHY EATING DIRECTIONS

Per serving Calories: 96

Total fat: 0g

Glycemic index: 0 g

Zero milligrams of cholesterol

Sodium: 2mg

Carbohydrates: 26g

Fiber: 5g

Phosphorus 0mg

Potassium: 198mg

1 g of protein

2nd stage of kidney disease

## 32. Savory Collard Chips

INGREDIENTS

1 bunch of collard greens

1 teaspoon of extra-virgin olive oil Juice of ½ lemon ½ teaspoon of garlic powder

COOK TIME: 20 MINUTES

If you like kale chips, you'll presumably cherish collard chips. The tough green holds up well to baking, making a fresh chip that is ideal for any time nibbling. The straightforward blend o f spices adds a garlicky kick to the chips, which will guarantee that you are getting a lot of vegetables in your eating routine regardless of whether they feel like vegetables.

¼ teaspoon of freshly ground black pepper

METHOD

Preheat the stove to 350°F. Line a baking sheet with material paper.

Cut the collards into 2-by-2-inch squares and wipe off with paper towels. In a huge bowl, throw the greens with the olive oil, lemon juice, garlic powder, and pepper. Utilize your hands to blend well, kneading the dressing into the greens until uniformly coated.

Arrange the collards in a solitary layer on the baking sheet, and cook for 8 minutes. Flip the pieces and cook for 8 extra minutes, until fresh. Eliminate from the stove, let cool, and store in an impermeable holder in a cool area for up to three days.

Substitution tip: If you like, utilize new garlic rather than dried. Mince 2 or 3 cloves, throw with the collards and continue as directed.

## HEALTHY EATING DIRECTIONS

Calories: 24 Total fat: 1g Glycemic index: 0 g Cholesterol: 0mg Sodium: 8mg Carbohydrates: 3g 1 gram of dietary fiber. Phosphorus 6mg Potassium: 72mg 1 g of protein

Kidney Disease Stage 1 INGREDIENTS

33. Roasted Red Pepper Hummus

COOK TIME: 10 MINUTES

Hummus is by and large viewed as a good food, yet like numerous other handled food varieties, locally acquired renditions are loaded up with sodium and additives. Simplify this hummus at home to hold sodium levels within proper limits, and keep the serving size to 2 tablespoons. This is simple in the event that you use it as a spread on sandwiches, or make vegetables the star and plunge them in hummus for a fast snack.

1 red bell pepper

(15-ounce) can chickpeas, drained and rinsed

Juice of 1 lemon

tablespoons of tahini

2 garlic cloves

2 tablespoons of extra-virgin olive oil

METHOD

Move a stove rack to the most noteworthy position. Heat the oven to high.

Core the pepper and cut it into three or four huge pieces. Orchestrate them on a baking sheet, skin-side up.

Broil the peppers for 5 to 10 minutes, until the skins are roasted. Eliminate from the stove and move the peppers to a little bowl. Cover with cling wrap and let them steam for 10 to 15 minutes, until sufficiently cool enough to handle.

Peel the singed skin off the peppers, and spot the peppers in a blender.

Add the chickpeas, lemon juice, tahini, garlic, and olive oil. Process until smooth, amounting to 1 tablespoon of water to change consistency as desired.

Substitution tip: This hummus can likewise be made without the red pepper whenever wanted. To do this, just follow Step 5. This will slice the potassium to 59mg per serving.

HEALTHY EATING DIRECTIONS

Per serving Calories: 103 Total fat: 6g

1 gram of saturated fat. Zero milligrams of cholesterol Carbohydrates: 10g Fiber: 3g

Protein: 3g Phosphorus 58mg Potassium: 91mg Sodium: 72mg

2nd stage of kidney disease

## 34. Thai-Style Eggplant Dip

SERVES 4 • PREP TIME: 10 MINUTES COOK TIME: 30 MINUTES In warm environments, for

example, Thailand, eggplant is

typical as a cooling vegetable with its sweet flavor. Here it's blended in with sweet, appetizing, and fiery components to make an awesome plunge that is perfect for vegetables or crackers.

INGREDIENTS

INGREDIENTS pound of Thai eggplant (or Japanese or Chinese eggplant) 2

tablespoons of rice vinegar 2

teaspoons of sugar 1teaspoon of low

sodium soy sauce

jalapeño pepper

garlic cloves

¼ cup of chopped basil

Cut vegetables or crackers, for serving

METHOD

Preheat the stove to 425°F.

Pierce the eggplant in a few spots with a stick or blade. Put on a rimmed baking sheet and cook until delicate, around 30 minutes. Let cool, cut down the middle, and scoop out the tissue of the eggplant into a blender.

Add the rice vinegar, sugar, soy sauce, jalapeño, garlic, and basil to the blender. Process until smooth. Present with cut vegetables or crackers.

Lower sodium tip: If you really want to bring down your sodium further, overlook the soy

sauce to bring down the sodium to 3mg.

HEALTHY EATING DIRECTIONS

Calories: 40 Total fat: 0g Glycemic index: 0 g Zero milligrams of cholesterol Carbohydrates: 10g Fiber: 4g

2 grams of protein Phosphorus 34mg Potassium: 284mg

End-Stage Renal Disease

## 35. Collard Salad Rolls with Peanut Dipping Sauce

SERVES 4 • PREP TIME: 20 MINUTES

These delectable Asian-motivated rolls permit you to inventively stack up on vegetables.

Amazing as an early afternoon nibble or light

lunch, the rolls have an awesome assortment of surfaces and flavor, and when dunked in

the sweet-and-zesty peanutbutter plunging sauce, they'll compensate you with a blast of taste.

INGREDIENTS FOR THE DIPPING SAUCE

¼ cup of peanut butter 2 tablespoons of honey Juice of 1 lime ¼ teaspoon of red chili flakes

FOR THE SALAD ROLLS

4 ounces of extra-firm tofu 1 bunch of collard greens

1 cup of thinly sliced purple cabbage 1 cup of bean sprouts 2 carrots, cut into matchsticks

½ cup of cilantro leaves and stems

METHOD TO MAKE THE DIPPING SAUCE

In a blender, join the peanut butter, honey, lime juice, and bean stew pieces, and interaction until smooth. Add 1 to 2 tablespoons of water as wanted for consistency.

TO MAKE THE SALAD ROLLS

Using paper towels, press the abundance dampness from the tofu. Cut into ½-inch-thick matchsticks.

Remove any intense stems from the collard greens and set aside.

Arrange every one of the fixings reachable. Cup one collard green leaf in your grasp, and add a few bits of the tofu and a limited quantity every one of the cabbage, bean sprouts, and carrots. Top with a few cilantro twigs, and roll into a chamber. Place each roll, crease side down,

on a serving platter while you collect the other rolls. Present with the plunging sauce. Substitution tip: To bring down the potassium, discard the cabbage and utilize just 1 carrot, which will drop the potassium to 208mg.

HEALTHY EATING DIRECTIONS

Calories: 174 Total

fat: 9g Saturated fat:

2g Cholesterol: 0mg

Carbohydrates: 20g Fiber:

5g

Protein: 8g Phosphorus

56mg Potassium: 284mg

Sodium: 42mg

Kidney Disease Stage 2 INGREDIENTS

36. Roasted Mint Carrots

SERVES 6 • PREP TIME: 5 MINUTES COOK TIME: 20 MINUTES

Carrots are an incredible wellspring of the cell reinforcement vitamin A, and albeit high in potassium, consumed with some restraint carrots can be a solid piece of your eating routine. In this planning, simmering normal pleasantness corresponding flavor. There are a few hundred assortments of carrots, yet search out those with the most profound orange tone, as they contain the most nutrient A.

improves the vegetable's

while mint adds a 1 pound of carrots, trimmed 1 tablespoon of extra-virgin olive oil Freshly ground black pepper

¼ cup of thinly sliced mint

METHOD

Preheat the broiler to 425°F.

Arrange the carrots in a solitary layer on a rimmed baking sheet. Sprinkle with the olive oil, and shake the carrots on the sheet to cover. Season with pepper.

Roast for 20 minutes, or until delicate and carmelized, mixing two times while cooking. Sprinkle with the mint and serve. Substitution tip: To bring down the potassium in this dish, utilize 8 ounces of carrots and 8 ounces of turnips cut into 3D squares. This will slice the potassium to 193mg.

HEALTHY EATING DIRECTIONS

Per serving Calories: 51 2 grams of total fat

Saturated fat: 4g Zero milligrams of cholesterol Carbohydrates: 7g 2 grams of fiber 1 g of protein Phosphorus 26mg Potassium: 242mg Sodium: 52mg

4th Stage of Kidney Failure

37. Roasted Root Vegetables

SERVES 6 • PREP TIME: 10 MINUTES COOK TIME: 25 MINUTES

Root vegetables have a solace food offer that makes them extraordinary for matching with, fish, and poultry dishes. Turnips, rutabaga, and parsnips may not be the main root vegetables you consider, yet these healthful forces to be reckoned with are well worth

exploring different avenues regarding. Simmering highlights their pleasantness, bringing about a delicate blend that is stacked in with flavor yet doesn't overpower the fundamental course.

Search for youthful and delicate vegetables-you don't have to strip them, so planning time is short.

## INGREDIENTS

1 cup of chopped turnips 1 cup of chopped rutabaga 1 cup of chopped parsnips

1 tablespoon of extra-virgin olive oil 1 teaspoon of fresh chopped rosemary Freshly ground black pepper

## METHOD

Preheat the stove to 400°F.

In a huge bowl, throw the turnips, rutabaga, and parsnips with the olive oil and rosemary. Orchestrate in a solitary layer on a baking sheet, and season with pepper.

Bake until the vegetables are delicate and seared, 20 to 25 minutes, mixing once. Replacement tip: Experiment with other new spices in this dish to suit your own preferences. Thyme, tarragon, oregano, and minced garlic all add exceptional flavors to these root vegetables.

## HEALTHY EATING DIRECTIONS

Per serving Nutritional Values: 52 calories per serving 2 grams of total fat

Glycemic index: 0 g Zero milligrams of cholesterol Carbohydrates: 7g 2 grams of fiber

1 g of protein Phosphorus 35mg

Potassium: 205mg Sodium: 22mg

## METHOD FOR DIAGNOSTIC OF KIDS WITH KIDS WITH KIDS WITH KIDS

Couscous with Vegetables (no. 38)

Serves 6 people • Preparation time: 10 minutes TIME TO PREPARE: 15 MINUTES

Couscous is a refined grain that cooks in a short amount of time, making it ideal for midweek dinners. Simply add the grain to a pot of boiling water, cover, and let sit for little short of 10 minutes, and voilà, this delightful grain is ready! This filling side dish, which is made up of vegetables, goes well with both fish and chicken dishes.

## INGREDIENTS

1 tablespoon extra-virgin olive oil (optional)

1 sweet onion, finely diced

carrots, peeled and diced

1 celery stalk, peeled and chopped

12 cup diced red or yellow bell peppers (optional)

I used a medium-sized zucchini, which I chopped.

Couscous is served in a cup.

Simple Chicken Broth or low-sodium store-bought chicken stock (about 12 cups total)

12 teaspoon of garlic powder is used in this recipe. peppercorns that are freshly ground

Heat the olive oil in a large skillet over a medium heat setting. Cook, stirring periodically, until the onion, carrot, celery, and chile pepper are soft.

In a large mixing bowl, combine the zucchini, couscous, stock, and garlic powder; stir well to combine. Heat until the mixture is boiling, stirring constantly. Immediately cover your head and get out of the heat. 5 to 8 minutes should enough. Pepper should be sprinkled on top after it has been cushioned with the fork. Use your imagination to create your own couscous by substituting different veggies. The zucchini may be replaced with yellow summer squash or pattypan squash. As an alternative to carrots and chile peppers, other vegetables such as asparagus, broccoli, or cauliflower may be used.

HEALTHY EATING DIRECTIONS

As a unit of measure, Nutritional Values: 154 Calories 3 grams of total fat

1 gram of saturated fat. Zero milligrams of cholesterol 27 g of carbohydrate Fiber:\s2g

5 grams of protein 83.3 mg of phosphorus K is 197 milligrams (mg). 36 milligrams of sodium

2nd stage of kidney disease

# Chapter Seven

# Rice with Garlic and Cauliflower

PREP TIME: 5 MINUTES • SERVES 8 PEOPLE 10 MINUTES FOR THE COOKING

Compared to white or brown rice, cauliflower rice is a shrewd vegetable-based alternative to these grains. Garlic and freshly ground dark pepper, in this form, combine to create a flavorful mixture that is ideal for recipes aimed at vegetable lovers. Because cauliflower has a significant amount of potassium, I recommend limiting the serving size to just one cup of cooked cauliflower.

Cup size: 12 oz (250 mL).

INGREDIENTS

cauliflower (1 medium head)

the extra-virgin olive oil (one tablespoon) minced 4 garlic cloves (peeled and peeled), peppercorns that are freshly ground

## METHOD

Remove the middle of the cauliflower with a sharp knife and cut the cauliflower into florets using the knife.

To make the florets into rice-sized pieces, pulse them in a food processor until they are the size of rice, being careful not to over-process them to the point of turning them mushy.

The olive oil should be heated in a large pan over medium heat. Mix in the garlic until it is barely aromatic, about 30 seconds.

Then, using a blender, cover the cauliflower. 1 tablespoon of water to the dish, cover, and reduce the heat to a medium setting Cook the cauliflower for 7 to 10 minutes, or until it is tender. Finish by seasoning with pepper.

Cooking tip: Cauliflower rice is delicious both when it is freshly prepared and after it has been allowed to rest in the refrigerator for a short period of time after preparation. Toss everything together in a clump and use it as a side dish throughout the week, reheating it in the microwave just before serving! The product can remain fresh for three to five days if stored in an impermeable container.

## HEALTHY EATING DIRECTIONS

As a unit of measure, The following number of calories is 37. 2 grams of total fat

Glycemic index: 0 g Zero milligrams of cholesterol 4 grams of carbohydrates 2 grams of fiber

2 grams of protein 355 milligrams of phosphorus Potassium:\s226mg 22.2 milligrams of sodium

4th Stage of Kidney Failure

Salad de Céléry et d'Arugula

• PREP TIME: 10 MINUTES • SERVES 4

When combined with the celery mash in this platter of mixed greens, the peppery arugula provides for a delicious contrast. Arugula is a bitter stomach companion that also happens to be a rich source of vitamins A and C, calcium, and folic acid. Consider the fact that sectors in the spring are connected to your hand

awesome

This company is open for business in the spring, late autumn, or at least tries.

achieving your individuality From seeds, you may grow arugula that will provide you with a large number of servings.

It takes no time at all to prepare mixed greens.

COMPONENTS OF A METHOD

1-inch-thick piece of shallot

Celery stalks (cut into 1-inch pieces about 1/4 inch thick) 3 celery leaves (cut into 1-inch pieces about 1/4 inch thick) 2 celery leaves (cut into 1-inch pieces about 1/4 inch thick)

cups of arugula that has been lightly compressed

extra-virgin olive oil (one tablespoon) 2

vinegar (white wine) in a tablespoon measuremen

peppercorns that are freshly ground

grated Parmesan cheese (about 2 tablespoons)

Toss the shallot, celery stalks, and arugula together in a medium-sized mixing basin until well combined.

In a small mixing bowl, whisk together the olive oil, vinegar, and pepper until well combined and smooth. Distribute the dressing over the platter of mixed greens, covering with plastic wrap. To serve, sprinkle the top with Parmesan cheese.

For a milder meal of mixed greens, you may replace an equal quantity of kid salad greens, or combine 1 cup of salad greens and 1 cup of arugula together in a blender or food processor.

HEALTHY EATING DIRECTIONS

calories per serving: 45 total fat grams per serving: 15

4g

1 gram of saturated fat.

2 milligrams of cholesterol

1 gram of carbohydrates Fiber:

0g

Phosphorus: 1 g protein

The following amounts of potassium are given: 47 milligrams Potassium

42mg of sodium

Stage 5 of kidney disease

salad with cucumbers and radishes (no. 41).

• PREP TIME: 10 MINUTES • SERVES 6 If you like the crunch of cucumbers and radishes, you'll enjoy this salad's crisp flavor and refreshing crunch! Despite the fact that these two vegetables are rich in potassium, it is necessary to limit the serving size to 12 cup. Use raw apple juice vinegar, which can be distinguished by the presence of cloudy silt at the bottom of the container, for the greatest taste and nutrition.

## INGREDIENTS

cucumbers, peeled and cut into two big pieces 1 bunch of radishes, cut 1 sweet onion, sliced 1 1/4 cup of apple cider vinegar the extra-virgin olive oil (one tablespoon) peppercorns that are freshly ground

## METHOD

Toss the cucumbers, radishes, and onion in a medium-sized mixing basin to combine them.

Cover the pan with the apple juice vinegar and olive oil and let it aside for 30 minutes. Pepper should be added towards the end of cooking. Making this platter of mixed greens ahead of time and storing it refrigerated in a sealed lid container until ready to serve is a good idea.

## HEALTHY EATING DIRECTIONS

As a unit of measure, Nutritional Values: 69 calories 8 grams of total fat

1 gram of saturated fat. Zero milligrams of cholesterol 8 g of carbohydrate 2 grams of fiber

2 grams of protein 50mg of phosphorus Potassium:\s386mg the amount of sodium in 29 milliliters.

Stage 4 of kidney disease METHOD

Salad de Spinach avec Vinaigrette d'Orange

PREP TIME: 5 MINUTES • SERVES 4 PEOPLE

It is a mother's day gift to yourself if you make this super-fast, revitalizing dish of mixed greens.

an endless supply of vitamins and minerals Some of its hidden medicinal benefits include the presence of vitamins A, C, K, and fiber. In order to ensure that the greens retain their firmness, prepare the dish of mixed greens with vinaigrette just before serving.

## INGREDIENTS

1 mandarin orange with its zest and juice

an extra-virgin olive oil of 1 tbsp

oil peppercorns that are freshly ground

6-ounces baby spinach (optional).

peel and membranes removed from two mandarin oranges.

In a small mixing bowl, whisk together the orange zest, orange juice, and olive oil until well combined and smooth. Pepper should be added towards the end of cooking.

A medium-sized mixing basin should include the spinach and orange chunks. Toss the dressed mixed greens into a large serving bowl and cover with plastic wrap. Serve. To produce a heartier and more self-sufficient dish of mixed greens for supper, add 1 cup of chopped avocado to the mixture. In this case, the fat material will increase to 9g, the phosphorus to 53 mg, and the potassium to 535 milligrams (mg).

## HEALTHY EATING DIRECTIONS

Calories per serving: 73 Total Calories

2 tablespoons oil (fat)

1 gram of saturated fat

Zero milligrams of cholesterol

10 grams of carbohydrates

2 grams of fiber

The following are the amounts of protein and phosphorus in grams: 2g.

The following amounts of potassium are given in milligrams (mg).

35.5 milligrams of sodium

## METHOD FOR DIAGNOSTIC OF KIDS WITH KIDS WITH KIDS WITH KIDS

Salad de légumes verts et de fruits de mer

• PREP TIME: 10 MINUTES • SERVES 4

There is no way to avoid being addicted to this sweet and savory combination of citrus, olives, and cranberries. When it comes to pepitas, which are hulled pumpkin seeds from a South and Central American kind of squash, they contain more protein than a variety of other nuts and seeds, and they offer a wonderful crunch to a portion of mixed greens. Because of their high protein content, the pepitas are combined with the cranberries and olives to create a pleasing combination of textures and tastes in this recipe.

INGREDIENTS

4 cups of salad greens (mixed)

fourteen-cup of pistachios

a lemon (with its juice)

extra virgin olive oil (about 2 tablespoons)

peppercorns that are freshly ground

Peel and finely slice 1 orange (or use a combination of oranges and lemons).

one and a quarter lemons, peeled and thinly sliced

1 14 cup dried cranberries (four tablespoons each)

Pitted Kalamata olives (1/4 cup): 4 teaspoons

Toss the greens, pepitas, lemon juice, and olive oil in a large mixing basin until everything is well distributed. Pepper should be added towards the end of cooking.

Place the greens on four dishes and garnish with 2 slices of orange and lemon on each plate, as desired. 1 tablespoon cranberries and 1 tablespoon Kalamata olives each dish, divided evenly. Serve.

A tasty addition to this mixed greens salad is the use of lightly toasted pepita seeds (see recipe below for more information). preheat the broiler to 25 degrees Fahrenheit in order to roast the almonds Pour 12 teaspoons of olive oil over the pepitas and lay them out on a baking sheet to dry out. Preheat the oven to 350°F and cook for 15 minutes, or until the potatoes are tender. Toss with the salad after allowing to cool. Use any citrus mixture in this serving of mixed greens to provide a variety of effects by substituting other citrus fruits. A variety of citrus fruits such as grapefruit, limes, and oranges may be used in any combination to suit your taste.

## HEALTHY EATING DIRECTIONS

As a unit of measure, Calories in a serving (142 calories) 9 grams of total fat 1 gram of saturated fat.

Zero milligrams of cholesterol Approximately 15 grams of carbohydrates 2 grams of fiber 3 grams of protein

116 milligrams of Phosphorus The following is the potassium content: 219 milligrams. Amount of sodium in one serving is 137 mg.

4th Stage of Kidney Failure

Roasted Beet Salad (number 44).

## INGREDIENTS

trimmings from 8 tiny beets

• PREP TIME: 15 MIN. • SERVES 4

10-MINUTE TIME SCHEDULE

PREP AND COOK TIME: 30 MIN

The sweetness of the veggies is enhanced when they are roasted, and when you consider how sweet the beet becomes after it is cooked, its taste is enhanced even more when it is boiled. Serve this debauched platter of mixed greens topped with feta and walnuts as a light lunch, or serve it with a heartier fowl dish for a heartier meal. When preparing this salad, use little beets since they cook more quickly and provide a beautiful visual display on the serving dish.

2 tablespoons of extra-virgin olive oil + 1 teaspoon extra-virgin olive oil, evenly distributed White wine vinegar (one tablespoon) is used in this recipe. mustard, 1 teaspoon of Dijon peppercorns that are freshly ground

Baby salad greens (about 4 cups total)

cut into slices a 12-inch sweet onion

2 tablespoons of feta cheese (crumbled) the walnut bits (about 2 tbsp.

METHOD

The stove should be preheated to 400 degrees Fahrenheit.

Cook the beets for 30 minutes, until they are fork-tender, after tossing them with 1 teaspoon of olive oil and wrapping them in foil.

The remaining 2 tablespoons of olive oil, vinegar, and mustard should be whisked together in a small bowl before using. Pepper should be added towards the end of cooking.

Combine the plate of mixed greens, onion, feta cheddar, and pecans in a medium-sized mixing bowl. Using approximately a quarter of the vinaigrette, dress the salad. Four plates should be used for this orchestration.

The beets are sliced and placed on top of the mixed greens to serve as a salad. The leftover dressing should be served as an accompaniment.

Tip: To prepare this serving of mixed greens ahead of time, simply combine the plate of mixed greens, onion, feta, and pecans in a bowl; do not toss it with the vinaigrette until you are ready to serve it, to avoid the greens becoming shriveled. Serve as soon as possible after storing in the refrigerator for up to three days.

HEALTHY EATING DIRECTIONS

170 calories per serving total calories

9g of fat

2 grams of saturated fat

4 milligrams of cholesterol.

20 grams of carbohydrates 5 grams of fiber Phosphorus: 4g Protein: 4g

Potassium: 585mg 93mg 93mg

217 milligrams of sodium

## METHOD FOR DIAGNOSTIC OF KIDS WITH KIDS WITH KIDS WITH KIDS

Salad de Poires et de Watercresse (45).

• PREP TIME: 10 MINUTES • SERVES 4

With a pungent flavor reminiscent of mustard, watercress is shockingly refreshing to the taste buds. This reviving fall salad, which includes pear, is practically a whirlwind of flavors. Use pears that retain their shape, such as Seckel, Comice, or Bosc, to achieve the best results possible.

## INGREDIENTS

quarter-cup of sweet onion, coarsely chopped

tablespoon Dijon mustard tablespoons extra-virgin olive oil a teaspoon of Dijon mustard White wine vinegar (one tablespoon) is used in this recipe.

Honey (about 1 teaspoon)

3 ounces watercress, thick stems removed, thoroughly washed Pears, cored and cut into wedges, 2 ripe pears

1.25 ounces of feta cheese crumbled

Combining all of the ingredients together in a food processor or blender will yield the best results. Continue to process until the mixture is completely smooth and uniform in color.

Watercress and dressing are combined in a medium-sized mixing bowl. Four plates should be used to organize your food. Using pear slices and crumbled feta cheese, garnish each serving.

Ingredient tip: Watercress has a short shelf life, so you'll want to use it up as soon as possible after preparing it. Pour water over the stems but do not submerge the leaves to store them. To prepare the leaves for utilization, wash them in a bowl of water, changing the water several times before depleting and utilizing the results.

## HEALTHY EATING DIRECTIONS

As a unit of measure, Nutritional Values: 120 calories 8 grams of total fat

Total fat: 4g Saturated fat 221 milligrams of cholesterol There are 3 grams of carbohydrates in this recipe. 0 grams of fiber

9 grams of protein 140mg of phosphorus K is 189 milligrams (mg). There are 93 milligrams of sodium in a teaspoon.

4th Stage of Kidney Failure

Meal Ideas for the Weeknight

Grilled Chicken with Rosemary

FOR 4 PEOPLE PREPARED TO EAT DUE DATE: JANUARY 12, 2019
A few fresh parsley leaves, finely chopped, are all you need for this dish.

Finely chop 1 tablespoon fresh rosemary (about 1 tablespoon total). Olive oil (about 1 tblsp. )

oil

4 boneless and skinless chicken breasts (approximately 4 ounces each) 5 oz.

crushed garlic cloves (chopped finely)

METHOD

Combine the salt, parsley, rosemary, olive oil, and garlic in a shallow and large mixing bowl. Marinate the chicken breasts for at least an hour in a bowl of spices before grilling them on the barbecue.

Preheat the barbecue to medium-high heat after greasing the grates. Barbecue chicken for 4 to 5 minutes per side, or until juices run clear and internal temperature of chicken reaches 168 degrees Fahrenheit, once the grill is hot and ready.

NUMBER OF CALORIES PER SERVING

Approximately 218 calories per serving There are 1g of carbohydrates in this recipe. Protein:\s34g

8 g of fats Phosphorus:\s267mg Potassium:\s440mg 560 milligrams of sodium

Stage 5 of kidney disease

## 52. Cauliflower Pilaf with Creamy Egg Scramble

METHOD OF SERVING: 3

25 MINUTES FOR THE COOKING

PREPARE THE INGREDIENTS: 1 medium onion, diced 2 heads of cauliflower (trimmed and coarsely chopped)

2 teaspoons chives, chopped 3 tablespoons olive oil, divided 4 eggs, salt and pepper to taste

For the cauliflower pilaf, heat 2 tablespoons oil in a large nonstick skillet over medium heat until hot. Cook the onions for about 10 minutes, or until they are delicate and transparent.

Prepare a bowl of rice finished cauliflower pilaf while processing cauliflower in a food processor, using the 'S' cutting edge, in the meantime.

To a container of onions, add the cauliflower pilaf and sauté until it is tender, about 5 to 10 minutes after the onions have been added. Blend in the pepper and seasonings until everything is smooth. Distribute the pilaf between two dishes in an even layer.

Cook remaining oil over a medium flame in a similar container.

Eggs, pepper to taste, and chives should be thoroughly mixed. Fry for a few minutes or until desired doneness is reached in hot oil. Using a spatula, divide the cauliflower pilaf into two portions and top each with an egg. Let's get this party started!

NUMBER OF CALORIES PER SERVING

Per serving, there are 250 calories. 10 grams of carbohydrates Protein:\s10g

20 g of fats Phosphorus:\s172mg Potassium:\s447mg 113 milligrams of sodium

4th Stage of Kidney Failure

Mediterranean-Style Roasted Veggies (number 53)

2 PEOPLE ARE SERVED

TIME ALLOWED FOR COOKING: 10 MIN

INGREDIENTS: 12 teaspoon freshly grated lemon zest (optional).

2 grape tomatoes (about 1 cup) the extra-virgin olive oil (one tablespoon)

lemon juice (about a tablespoon) dried oregano (about 1 teaspoon) 10 pitted black olives, sliced 12 ounces broccoli crowns, trimmed and cut into bite-sized pieces 10 pitted black olives, sliced crushed garlic cloves (chopped finely) rinsed capers 2 teaspoons capers 2 teaspoons capers

## METHOD

Prepare a baking sheet by spraying it with cooking oil and preheating the oven to 350oF.

Combine the salt, garlic, oil, tomatoes, and broccoli in a large mixing bowl until everything is completely covered. Cook for 8 to 10 minutes after spreading broccoli on a baking sheet that has been prepared in advance.

3 - In a large mixing bowl, combine the escapades, oregano leaves, olives, lime juice, and lemon zest. Cooked vegetables should be added last, so serve while they are still hot.

## NUMBER OF CALORIES PER SERVING

Per serving, there are 110 calories and 16 grams of carbohydrates.

6 grams of protein 4 g of fats 138 milligrams of phosphorus. Potassium:\s745mg

KD Stage 5 sodium intake is 214 mg per day.

# Chapter Eight

# Garden Lettuce Salad with Fresh ruit

THERE ARE 4 SERVINGS:

TIME TO COMPLETE COOKING: 0 MIN

COMPOSITION: 1 cup apple cider vinegar, 1 cup brown sugar

13/4 cup almonds, finely chopped

12 avocados, thinly sliced 12 cup extra virgin olive oil 1 teaspoon cumin

oil of rapeseed

one and a half lemons, freshly squeezed

spoonful bla pepper, freshly ground

tablespoons grainy mustard 2 Granny Smith apples, thinly sliced 6-cups of lettuce, thinly sliced

METHOD

Prepare lemon juice and apples in a large salad bowl filled with mixed greens. Combine the almonds, avocado, and lettuce in a blender until well-incorporated.

A small mixing bowl can be used to combine all of the ingredients except the olive oil until the salt is completely dissolved.

Using your hands, toss the dressing over the lettuce mixture to combine it. Let's get this party started!

NUMBER OF CALORIES PER SERVING

Each serving has 123 calories. 16.5 g of carbs

2 grams of protein 6 g of fats

Potassium is 56 milligrams. the following amount of potassium is consumed: 450mg 35.5 milligrams of sodium

Symptoms of Stage 1 Kidney Disease

Salad de Coleslaw avec pommes de terre (55.

INGREDIENTS

red cabbage shreds in a cup or two

12 cup shredded carrots and 14 cup finely chopped scallions are used in this recipe. 2 lemons squeezed into a cup

Honey (one tablespoon)

the extra-virgin olive oil (one tablespoon)

peeled and finely chopped 1 large tart apple (about 1 cup) peppercorns that are freshly ground

## METHOD

• PREP TIME: 10 MINUTES • SERVES 4

A stalwart vegetable that is rich in cancer-fighting antioxidants as well as antibacterial, antiviral, and cell-reinforcing properties, cabbage is mind-boggling when eaten raw. A tart apple and the red-cabbage assortment (which is particularly high in cell reinforcements) combine to create a remarkable combination in this coleslaw. Serve this plate of mixed greens alongside roasted poultry, pork, or fish to make a complete meal.

Mix together the cabbage, carrots, scallions, lemon juice, honey, olive oil, and apple in a large mixing bowl until well-combined. To chill for 30 minutes, combine all of the ingredients in a blender until smooth. Just before serving, sprinkle with black pepper.

Tips for using cabbage: Cabbage is available in both red and green colors. Because you will only need half a head of cabbage for this recipe, assuming your grocery store sells split and wrapped cabbage, you can purchase this to avoid wasting food. Purchased pre-destroyed cabbage, on the other hand, can save you time in the kitchen.

## HEALTHY EATING DIRECTIONS

Amount of calories in a single serving: 94 4 grams of total fat The following is the amount of saturated fat: 1 gram

Zero milligrams of cholesterol There are 16 grams of carbohydrate in total. 3 grams of fiber 2 grams of protein

Calcium: 28 milligrams (mg) K is 303 milligrams (mg). 281 milligrams of sodium

Symptoms of Stage 1 Kidney Disease

A Salad of Roasted Cauliflower and Mixed Greens (see recipe #56).

PREP TIME: 10 MIN INGREDIENTS SERVES 4 DIRECTIONS:

TIME TO PREPARE: 35 MINUTES TIME TO COOK

Whatever you throw at mixed child salad greens, they'll handle it with ease. When combined with cauliflower, these lightly seasoned greens make a stunning display on a simple plate of mixed greens, with only one other vegetable taking precedence. Cooked until golden brown, the delicate cauliflower florets are accompanied by a light vinaigrette and a sprinkling of pecan pieces for added surface area and protein in this elegant supper accompaniment.

cauliflower (small head, cut into small florets): 1 cup extra-virgin olive oil, divided into 2 tablespoons peppercorns that are freshly ground

6 ounces of baby salad greens in a variety of colors. the walnut bits (about 2 tbsp.

Apple cider vinegar (about 1 tablespoon)

METHOD

Preheat the oven to 400 degrees Fahrenheit.

Cauliflower and 1 tablespoon of olive oil are combined in a large mixing bowl. Pepper should be added towards the end of cooking. Make a single layer on a large baking sheet and arrange the orchestration.

Stirring occasionally, cook for 30 to 35 minutes, until delicate and brilliant brown, blending several times along the way. Allow for a 10-minute cooling period.

Meanwhile, combine the remaining tablespoon of olive oil with the vinegar in a small mixing bowl.

Mix together the mixed greens, pecans, and cauliflower in a large mixing bowl until well combined. Mix in the olive oil and vinegar mixture just before serving, and season with pepper if necessary.

Cooking tip: Make extra broiled cauliflower to serve as a side dish and keep some on hand so you can quickly whip up this plate of mixed greens when you're hungry. Three to five days will be sufficient storage time in an impermeable compartment of a cooler.

HEALTHY EATING DIRECTIONS

Caloric Value per Serving: 108 Glycemic Index: 9 grams

The following is the amount of saturated fat: 1 gram Zero milligrams of cholesterol 5 grams of carbohydrates 2 grams of fiber 2 grams of protein Phosphorus:\s42mg The following is the potassium content: 217 milligrams 50 milligrams of sodium

4th Stage of Kidney Failure

Salad de Bulgur et de Brocoli (57).

TIME TO PREPARE FOR SERVES 4: 10 MIN 15 MINUTES FOR THE COOKING

Despite the fact that mint is playing a supporting role here, this refreshing spice brings out the best in everything it comes into contact with. Here, the mint is combined with lemon, broccoli, and cherry tomatoes to create a vibrantly seasoned serving of mixed greens, which is anchored by nutty-tasting bulgur. Serve this plate of mixed greens on its own or spoon it into a salad dressing.

Make a delectable active plate of mixed greens wrap with colossal lettuce leaves.

INGREDIENTS

3-cups of chopped broccoli florets 1 cup of chopped cauliflower

Bulgur in a cup

2 cherry tomatoes, halved (12 cup total)

sunflower seeds (raw) in a quarter cup

chopped mint leaves (about a quarter cup) a lemon (with its juice) the extra-virgin olive oil (one tablespoon)

METHOD

Fill a medium-sized bowl halfway with ice and water and set up an ice-water shower in it.

Almost completely fill a medium-sized pot with water and bring it up to a boil. Trim and blanche 3 minutes with the broccoli. Toss the broccoli into the ice shower with an open spoon while maintaining control over the temperature of the cooking water. After approximately 3 minutes of cooling, channel the ice and water through a channeling machine. Separate the broccoli from the rest of the vegetables.

To prepare the bulgur, add it to the boiling water and remove it from the heat. Cover and set aside for 15 minutes. Create a channel in the bulgur by squeezing it with the back of the spoon to remove any excess water.

Toss the broccoli, bulgur, tomatoes, sunflower seeds, mint, lemon juice, and olive oil in a medium-sized mixing bowl until well combined. Make a quick meal of it. Repair tip: Bulgur can smell bad quickly, so buy only what you will use right away rather than letting it sit around. Check for freshness by smelling it before purchasing and storing it in the refrigerator if at all possible.

## HEALTHY EATING DIRECTIONS

Caloric Value per Serving: 156 6 grams of total fat

The following is the amount of saturated fat: 1 gram Zero milligrams of cholesterol Contains 24 grams of carbohydrates. Fiber:\s7g

6 grams of protein Phosphorus:\s101mg Potassium:\s315mg 21.1 milligrams of sodium

Symptoms of Stage 1 Kidney DiseaseMETHOD

The stove should be preheated to 400 degrees Fahrenheit.

Cook the beets for 30 minutes, until they are fork-tender, after tossing them with 1 teaspoon of olive oil and wrapping them in foil.

The remaining 2 tablespoons of olive oil, vinegar, and mustard should be whisked together in a small bowl before using. Pepper should be added towards the end of cooking.

Combine the plate of mixed greens, onion, feta cheddar, and pecans in a medium-sized mixing bowl. Using approximately a quarter of the vinaigrette, dress the salad. Four plates should be used for this orchestration.

The beets are sliced and placed on top of the mixed greens to serve as a salad. The leftover dressing should be served as an accompaniment.

Tip: To prepare this serving of mixed greens ahead of time, simply combine the plate of mixed greens, onion, feta, and pecans in a bowl; do not toss it with the vinaigrette until you are ready to serve it, to avoid the greens becoming shriveled. Serve as soon as possible after storing in the refrigerator for up to three days.

HEALTHY EATING DIRECTIONS

170 calories per serving total calories

9g of fat

2 grams of saturated fat

4 milligrams of cholesterol.

20 grams of carbohydrates 5 grams of fiber Phosphorus: 4g Protein: 4g

Potassium: 585mg 93mg 93mg

217 milligrams of sodiu

METHOD FOR DIAGNOSTIC OF KIDS WITH KIDS WITH KIDS WITH KIDS

Salad de Poires et de Watercresse (45).

• PREP TIME: 10 MINUTES • SERVES 4

With a pungent flavor reminiscent of mustard, watercress is shockingly refreshing to the taste buds. This reviving fall salad, which includes pear, is practically a whirlwind of flavors. Use pears that retain their shape, such as Seckel, Comice, or Bosc, to achieve the best results possible.

## INGREDIENTS

quarter-cup of sweet onion, coarsely chopped

tablespoon Dijon mustard tablespoons extra-virgin olive oil a teaspoon of Dijon mustard White wine vinegar (one tablespoon) is used in this recipe.

Honey (about 1 teaspoon)

3 ounces watercress, thick stems removed, thoroughly washed Pears, cored and cut into wedges, 2 ripe pears

1.25 ounces of feta cheese crumbled

Combining all of the ingredients together in a food processor or blender will yield the best results. Continue to process until the mixture is completely smooth and uniform in color.

Watercress and dressing are combined in a medium-sized mixing bowl. Four plates should be used to organize your food. Using pear slices and crumbled feta cheese, garnish each serving.

Ingredient tip: Watercress has a short shelf life, so you'll want to use it up as soon as possible after preparing it. Pour water over the stems but do not submerge the leaves to store them. To prepare the leaves for utilization, wash them in a bowl of water, changing the water several times before depleting and utilizing the results.

## HEALTHY EATING DIRECTIONS

As a unit of measure, Nutritional Values: 120 calories 8 grams of total fat

Total fat: 4g Saturated fat 221 milligrams of cholesterol There are 3 grams of carbohydrates in this recipe. 0 grams of fiber

9 grams of protein 140mg of phosphorus K is 189 milligrams (mg). There are 93 milligrams of sodium in a teaspoon.

4th Stage of Kidney Failure

Meal Ideas for the Weeknight

Grilled Chicken with Rosemary

FOR 4 PEOPLE PREPARED TO EAT DUE DATE: JANUARY 12, 2019 A few fresh parsley leaves, finely chopped, are all you need for this dish.

Finely chop 1 tablespoon fresh rosemary (about 1 tablespoon total). Olive oil (about 1 tblsp. )

oil

4 boneless and skinless chicken breasts (approximately 4 ounces each) 5 oz.

crushed garlic cloves (chopped finely)

## METHOD

Combine the salt, parsley, rosemary, olive oil, and garlic in a shallow and large mixing bowl. Marinate the chicken breasts for at least an hour in a bowl of spices before grilling them on the barbecue.

Preheat the barbecue to medium-high heat after greasing the grates. Barbecue chicken for 4 to 5 minutes per side, or until juices run clear and internal temperature of chicken reaches 168 degrees Fahrenheit, once the grill is hot and ready.

## NUMBER OF CALORIES PER SERVING

Approximately 218 calories per serving There are 1g of carbohydrates in this recipe. Protein:\s34g

8 g of fats Phosphorus:\s267mg Potassium:\s440mg 560 milligrams of sodium

Stage 5 of kidney disease

52. Cauliflower Pilaf with Creamy Egg Scramble

METHOD OF SERVING: 3

25 MINUTES FOR THE COOKING

PREPARE THE INGREDIENTS: 1 medium onion, diced 2 heads of cauliflower (trimmed and coarsely chopped)

2 teaspoons chives, chopped 3 tablespoons olive oil, divided 4 eggs, salt and pepper to taste

For the cauliflower pilaf, heat 2 tablespoons oil in a large nonstick skillet over medium heat until hot. Cook the onions for about 10 minutes, or until they are delicate and transparent.

Prepare a bowl of rice finished cauliflower pilaf while processing cauliflower in a food processor, using the 'S' cutting edge, in the meantime.

To a container of onions, add the cauliflower pilaf and sauté until it is tender, about 5 to 10 minutes after the onions have been added. Blend in the pepper and seasonings until everything is smooth. Distribute the pilaf between two dishes in an even layer.

Cook remaining oil over a medium flame in a similar container.

Eggs, pepper to taste, and chives should be thoroughly mixed. Fry for a few minutes or until desired doneness is reached in hot oil. Using a spatula, divide the cauliflower pilaf into two portions and top each with an egg. Let's get this party started!

NUMBER OF CALORIES PER SERVING

Per serving, there are 250 calories. 10 grams of carbohydrates Protein:\s10g

20 g of fats Phosphorus:\s172mg Potassium:\s447mg 113 milligrams of sodium

4th Stage of Kidney Failure

Mediterranean-Style Roasted Veggies (number 53)

2 PEOPLE ARE SERVED

TIME ALLOWED FOR COOKING: 10 MIN

INGREDIENTS: 12 teaspoon freshly grated lemon zest (optional).

2 grape tomatoes (about 1 cup) the extra-virgin olive oil (one tablespoon)

lemon juice (about a tablespoon) dried oregano (about 1 teaspoon) 10 pitted black olives, sliced 12 ounces broccoli crowns, trimmed and cut into bite-sized pieces 10 pitted black olives, sliced

crushed garlic cloves (chopped finely) rinsed capers 2 teaspoons capers 2 teaspoons capers

METHOD

Prepare a baking sheet by spraying it with cooking oil and preheating the oven to 350oF.

Combine the salt, garlic, oil, tomatoes, and broccoli in a large mixing bowl until everything is completely covered. Cook for 8 to 10 minutes after spreading broccoli on a baking sheet that has been prepared in advance.

3 - In a large mixing bowl, combine the escapades, oregano leaves, olives, lime juice, and lemon zest. Cooked vegetables should be added last, so serve while they are still hot.

## NUMBER OF CALORIES PER SERVING

Per serving, there are 110 calories and 16 grams of carbohydrates.

6 grams of protein 4 g of fats 138 milligrams of phosphorus. Potassium:\s745mg

KD Stage 5 sodium intake is 214 mg per day.

Garden Lettuce Salad with Fresh Fruit

THERE ARE 4 SERVINGS:

TIME TO COMPLETE COOKING: 0 MIN

COMPOSITION: 1 cup apple cider vinegar, 1 cup brown sugar

13/4 cup almonds, finely chopped

12 avocados, thinly sliced 12 cup extra virgin olive oil 1 teaspoon cumin

oil of rapeseed

one and a half lemons, freshly squeezed

spoonful bla pepper, freshly ground

tablespoons grainy mustard 2 Granny Smith apples, thinly sliced 6-cups of lettuce, thinly sliced

METHOD

Prepare lemon juice and apples in a large salad bowl filled with mixed greens. Combine the almonds, avocado, and lettuce in a blender until well-incorporated.

A small mixing bowl can be used to combine all of the ingredients except the olive oil until the salt is completely dissolved.

Using your hands, toss the dressing over the lettuce mixture to combine it. Let's get this party started!

NUMBER OF CALORIES PER SERVING

Each serving has 123 calories. 16.5 g of carbs

2 grams of protein 6 g of fats

Potassium is 56 milligrams. the following amount of potassium is consumed: 450mg 35.5 milligrams of sodium

Symptoms of Stage 1 Kidney Disease

Salad de Coleslaw avec pommes de terre (55.

INGREDIENTS

red cabbage shreds in a cup or two

12 cup shredded carrots and 14 cup finely chopped scallions are used in this recipe. 2 lemons squeezed into a cup

Honey (one tablespoon)

the extra-virgin olive oil (one tablespoon)

peeled and finely chopped 1 large tart apple (about 1 cup) peppercorns that are freshly ground

METHOD

• PREP TIME: 10 MINUTES • SERVES 4

A stalwart vegetable that is rich in cancer-fighting antioxidants as well as antibacterial, antiviral, and cell-reinforcing properties, cabbage is mind-boggling when eaten raw. A tart apple and the red-cabbage assortment (which is particularly high in cell reinforcements) combine to create a remarkable combination in this coleslaw. Serve this plate of mixed greens alongside roasted poultry, pork, or fish to make a complete meal.

Mix together the cabbage, carrots, scallions, lemon juice, honey, olive oil, and apple in a large mixing bowl until well-combined. To chill for 30 minutes, combine all of the ingredients in a blender until smooth. Just before serving, sprinkle with black pepper.

Tips for using cabbage: Cabbage is available in both red and green colors. Because you will only need half a head of cabbage for this recipe, assuming your grocery store sells split and wrapped cabbage, you can purchase this to avoid wasting food. Purchased pre-destroyed cabbage, on the other hand, can save you time in the kitchen.

## HEALTHY EATING DIRECTIONS

Amount of calories in a single serving: 94 4 grams of total fat The following is the amount of saturated fat: 1 gram

Zero milligrams of cholesterol There are 16 grams of carbohydrate in total. 3 grams of fiber 2 grams of protein

Calcium: 28 milligrams (mg) K is 303 milligrams (mg). 281 milligrams of sodium

Symptoms of Stage 1 Kidney Disease

# A Salad of Roasted Cauliflower and Mixed Greens

PREP TIME: 10 MIN INGREDIENTS SERVES 4 DIRECTIONS:

TIME TO PREPARE: 35 MINUTES TIME TO COOK

Whatever you throw at mixed child salad greens, they'll handle it with ease. When combined with cauliflower, these lightly seasoned greens make a stunning display on a simple plate of mixed greens, with only one other vegetable taking precedence. Cooked until golden brown, the delicate cauliflower florets are accompanied by a light vinaigrette and a sprinkling of pecan pieces for added surface area and protein in this elegant supper accompaniment.

cauliflower (small head, cut into small florets): 1 cup extra-virgin olive oil, divided into 2 tablespoons peppercorns that are freshly ground

6 ounces of baby salad greens in a variety of colors. the walnut bits (about 2 tbsp.

Apple cider vinegar (about 1 tablespoon)

## METHOD

Preheat the oven to 400 degrees Fahrenheit.

Cauliflower and 1 tablespoon of olive oil are combined in a large mixing bowl. Pepper should be added towards the end of cooking. Make a single layer on a large baking sheet and arrange the orchestration.

Stirring occasionally, cook for 30 to 35 minutes, until delicate and brilliant brown, blending several times along the way. Allow for a 10-minute cooling period.

Meanwhile, combine the remaining tablespoon of olive oil with the vinegar in a small mixing bowl.

Mix together the mixed greens, pecans, and cauliflower in a large mixing bowl until well combined. Mix in the olive oil and vinegar mixture just before serving, and season with pepper if necessary.

Cooking tip: Make extra broiled cauliflower to serve as a side dish and keep some on hand so you can quickly whip up this plate of mixed greens when you're hungry. Three to five days will be sufficient storage time in an impermeable compartment of a cooler.

## HEALTHY EATING DIRECTIONS

Caloric Value per Serving: 108 Glycemic Index: 9 grams

The following is the amount of saturated fat: 1 gram Zero milligrams of cholesterol 5 grams of carbohydrates 2 grams of fiber 2 grams of protein Phosphorus:\s42mg The following is the potassium content: 217 milligrams 50 milligrams of sodium

## 4th Stage of Kidney Failure

Salad de Bulgur et de Brocoli (57).

TIME TO PREPARE FOR SERVES 4: 10 MIN 15 MINUTES FOR THE COOKING

Despite the fact that mint is playing a supporting role here, this refreshing spice brings out the best in everything it comes into contact with. Here, the mint is combined with lemon, broccoli, and cherry tomatoes to create a vibrantly seasoned serving of mixed greens, which is anchored by nutty-tasting bulgur. Serve this plate of mixed greens on its own or spoon it into a salad dressing.

Make a delectable active plate of mixed greens wrap with colossal lettuce leaves.

INGREDIENTS

3-cups of chopped broccoli florets 1 cup of chopped cauliflower

Bulgur in a cup

2 cherry tomatoes, halved (12 cup total)

sunflower seeds (raw) in a quarter cup

chopped mint leaves (about a quarter cup) a lemon (with its juice) the extra-virgin olive oil (one tablespoon)

METHOD

Fill a medium-sized bowl halfway with ice and water and set up an ice-water shower in it.

Almost completely fill a medium-sized pot with water and bring it up to a boil. Trim and blanche 3 minutes with the broccoli. Toss the broccoli into the ice shower with an open spoon while maintaining control over the temperature of the cooking water. After approximately 3 minutes of cooling, channel the ice and water through a channeling machine. Separate the broccoli from the rest of the vegetables.

To prepare the bulgur, add it to the boiling water and remove it from the heat. Cover and set aside for 15 minutes. Create a channel in the bulgur by squeezing it with the back of the spoon to remove any excess water.

Toss the broccoli, bulgur, tomatoes, sunflower seeds, mint, lemon juice, and olive oil in a medium-sized mixing bowl until well combined. Make a quick meal of it. Repair tip: Bulgur can smell bad quickly, so buy only what you will use right away rather than letting it sit around. Check for freshness by smelling it before purchasing and storing it in the refrigerator if at all possible.

HEALTHY EATING DIRECTIONS

Caloric Value per Serving: 156 6 grams of total fat

The following is the amount of saturated fat: 1 gram Zero milligrams of cholesterol Contains 24 grams of carbohydrates. Fiber:\s7g

6 grams of protein Phosphorus:\s101mg Potassium:\s315mg 21.1 milligrams of sodium

Symptoms of Stage 1 Kidney DiseaseMETHOD

The stove should be preheated to 400 degrees Fahrenheit.

Cook the beets for 30 minutes, until they are fork-tender, after tossing them with 1 teaspoon of olive oil and wrapping them in foil.

The remaining 2 tablespoons of olive oil, vinegar, and mustard should be whisked together in a small bowl before using. Pepper should be added towards the end of cooking.

Combine the plate of mixed greens, onion, feta cheddar, and pecans in a medium-sized mixing bowl. Using approximately a quarter of the vinaigrette, dress the salad. Four plates should be used for this orchestration.

The beets are sliced and placed on top of the mixed greens to serve as a salad. The leftover dressing should be served as an accompaniment.

Tip: To prepare this serving of mixed greens ahead of time, simply combine the plate of mixed greens, onion, feta, and pecans in a bowl; do not toss it with the vinaigrette until you are ready to serve it, to avoid the greens becoming shriveled. Serve as soon as possible after storing in the refrigerator for up to three days.

HEALTHY EATING DIRECTIONS

170 calories per serving total calories

9g of fat

2 grams of saturated fat

4 milligrams of cholesterol.

20 grams of carbohydrates 5 grams of fiber Phosphorus: 4g Protein: 4g

Potassium: 585mg 93mg 93mg

217 milligrams of sodium

METHOD FOR DIAGNOSTIC OF KIDS WITH KIDS WITH KIDS WITH KIDS

Salad de Poires et de Watercresse (45).

• PREP TIME: 10 MINUTES • SERVES 4

With a pungent flavor reminiscent of mustard, watercress is shockingly refreshing to the taste buds. This reviving fall salad, which includes pear, is practically a whirlwind of flavors. Use pears that retain their shape, such as Seckel, Comice, or Bosc, to achieve the best results possible.

INGREDIENTS

quarter-cup of sweet onion, coarsely chopped

tablespoon Dijon mustard tablespoons extra-virgin olive oil a teaspoon of Dijon mustard White wine vinegar (one tablespoon) is used in this recipe.

Honey (about 1 teaspoon)

3 ounces watercress, thick stems removed, thoroughly washed Pears, cored and cut into wedges, 2 ripe pears

1.25 ounces of feta cheese crumbled

Combining all of the ingredients together in a food processor or blender will yield the best results. Continue to process until the mixture is completely smooth and uniform in color.

Watercress and dressing are combined in a medium-sized mixing bowl. Four plates should be used to organize your food. Using pear slices and crumbled feta cheese, garnish each serving.

Ingredient tip: Watercress has a short shelf life, so you'll want to use it up as soon as possible after preparing it. Pour water over the stems but do not submerge the leaves to store them. To prepare the leaves for utilization, wash them in a bowl of water, changing the water several times before depleting and utilizing the results.

## HEALTHY EATING DIRECTIONS

As a unit of measure, Nutritional Values: 120 calories 8 grams of total fat

Total fat: 4g Saturated fat 221 milligrams of cholesterol There are 3 grams of carbohydrates in this recipe. 0 grams of fiber

9 grams of protein 140mg of phosphorus K is 189 milligrams (mg). There are 93 milligrams of sodium in a teaspoon.

4th Stage of Kidney Failure

Meal Ideas for the Weeknight

Grilled Chicken with Rosemary

FOR 4 PEOPLE PREPARED TO EAT DUE DATE: JANUARY 12, 2019 A few fresh parsley leaves, finely chopped, are all you need for this dish.

Finely chop 1 tablespoon fresh rosemary (about 1 tablespoon total). Olive oil (about 1 tblsp. )

oil

4 boneless and skinless chicken breasts (approximately 4 ounces each) 5 oz.

crushed garlic cloves (chopped finely)

METHOD

Combine the salt, parsley, rosemary, olive oil, and garlic in a shallow and large mixing bowl. Marinate the chicken breasts for at least an hour in a bowl of spices before grilling them on the barbecue.

Preheat the barbecue to medium-high heat after greasing the grates. Barbecue chicken for 4 to 5 minutes per side, or until juices run clear and internal temperature of chicken reaches 168 degrees Fahrenheit, once the grill is hot and ready.

NUMBER OF CALORIES PER SERVING

Approximately 218 calories per serving There are 1g of carbohydrates in this recipe. Protein:\s34g

8 g of fats Phosphorus:\s267mg Potassium:\s440mg 560 milligrams of sodium

Stage 5 of kidney disease

52. Cauliflower Pilaf with Creamy Egg Scramble

METHOD OF SERVING: 3

25 MINUTES FOR THE COOKING

PREPARE THE INGREDIENTS: 1 medium onion, diced 2 heads of cauliflower (trimmed and coarsely chopped)

2 teaspoons chives, chopped 3 tablespoons olive oil, divided 4 eggs, salt and pepper to taste

For the cauliflower pilaf, heat 2 tablespoons oil in a large nonstick skillet over medium heat until hot. Cook the onions for about 10 minutes, or until they are delicate and transparent.

Prepare a bowl of rice finished cauliflower pilaf while processing cauliflower in a food processor, using the 'S' cutting edge, in the meantime.

To a container of onions, add the cauliflower pilaf and sauté until it is tender, about 5 to 10 minutes after the onions have been added. Blend in the pepper and seasonings until everything is smooth. Distribute the pilaf between two dishes in an even layer.

Cook remaining oil over a medium flame in a similar container.

Eggs, pepper to taste, and chives should be thoroughly mixed. Fry for a few minutes or until desired doneness is reached in hot oil. Using a spatula, divide the cauliflower pilaf into two portions and top each with an egg. Let's get this party started!

NUMBER OF CALORIES PER SERVING

Per serving, there are 250 calories. 10 grams of carbohydrates Protein:\s10g

20 g of fats Phosphorus:\s172mg Potassium:\s447mg 113 milligrams of sodium

4th Stage of Kidney Failure

Mediterranean-Style Roasted Veggies (number 53)

2 PEOPLE ARE SERVED

TIME ALLOWED FOR COOKING: 10 MIN

INGREDIENTS: 12 teaspoon freshly grated lemon zest (optional).

2 grape tomatoes (about 1 cup) the extra-virgin olive oil (one tablespoon)

lemon juice (about a tablespoon) dried oregano (about 1 teaspoon) 10 pitted black olives, sliced 12 ounces broccoli crowns, trimmed and cut into bite-sized pieces 10 pitted black olives, sliced

crushed garlic cloves (chopped finely) rinsed capers 2 teaspoons capers 2 teaspoons capers

METHOD

Prepare a baking sheet by spraying it with cooking oil and preheating the oven to 350oF.

Combine the salt, garlic, oil, tomatoes, and broccoli in a large mixing bowl until everything is completely covered. Cook for 8 to 10 minutes after spreading broccoli on a baking sheet that has been prepared in advance.

3 - In a large mixing bowl, combine the escapades, oregano leaves, olives, lime juice, and lemon zest. Cooked vegetables should be added last, so serve while they are still hot.

## NUMBER OF CALORIES PER SERVING

Per serving, there are 110 calories and 16 grams of carbohydrates.

6 grams of protein 4 g of fats 138 milligrams of phosphorus. Potassium:\s745mg

KD Stage 5 sodium intake is 214 mg per day.

Garden Lettuce Salad with Fresh Fruit

THERE ARE 4 SERVINGS:

TIME TO COMPLETE COOKING: 0 MIN

COMPOSITION: 1 cup apple cider vinegar, 1 cup brown sugar

13/4 cup almonds, finely chopped

12 avocados, thinly sliced 12 cup extra virgin olive oil 1 teaspoon cumin

oil of rapeseed

one and a half lemons, freshly squeezed

spoonful bla pepper, freshly ground

tablespoons grainy mustard 2 Granny Smith apples, thinly sliced 6-cups of lettuce, thinly sliced

METHOD

Prepare lemon juice and apples in a large salad bowl filled with mixed greens. Combine the almonds, avocado, and lettuce in a blender until well-incorporated.

A small mixing bowl can be used to combine all of the ingredients except the olive oil until the salt is completely dissolved.

Using your hands, toss the dressing over the lettuce mixture to combine it. Let's get this party started!

NUMBER OF CALORIES PER SERVING

Each serving has 123 calories. 16.5 g of carbs

2 grams of protein 6 g of fats

Potassium is 56 milligrams. the following amount of potassium is consumed: 450mg 35.5 milligrams of sodium

Symptoms of Stage 1 Kidney Disease

Salad de Coleslaw avec pommes de terre (55.

INGREDIENTS

red cabbage shreds in a cup or two

12 cup shredded carrots and 14 cup finely chopped scallions are used in this recipe. 2 lemons squeezed into a cup

Honey (one tablespoon)

the extra-virgin olive oil (one tablespoon)

peeled and finely chopped 1 large tart apple (about 1 cup) peppercorns that are freshly ground

## METHOD

• PREP TIME: 10 MINUTES • SERVES 4

A stalwart vegetable that is rich in cancer-fighting antioxidants as well as antibacterial, antiviral, and cell-reinforcing properties, cabbage is mind-boggling when eaten raw. A tart apple and the red-cabbage assortment (which is particularly high in cell reinforcements) combine to create a remarkable combination in this coleslaw. Serve this plate of mixed greens alongside roasted poultry, pork, or fish to make a complete meal.

Mix together the cabbage, carrots, scallions, lemon juice, honey, olive oil, and apple in a large mixing bowl until well-combined. To chill for 30 minutes, combine all of the ingredients in a blender until smooth. Just before serving, sprinkle with black pepper.

Tips for using cabbage: Cabbage is available in both red and green colors. Because you will only need half a head of cabbage for this recipe, assuming your grocery store sells split and wrapped cabbage, you can purchase this to avoid wasting food. Purchased pre-destroyed cabbage, on the other hand, can save you time in the kitchen.

## HEALTHY EATING DIRECTIONS

Amount of calories in a single serving: 94 4 grams of total fat The following is the amount of saturated fat: 1 gram

Zero milligrams of cholesterol There are 16 grams of carbohydrate in total. 3 grams of fiber 2 grams of protein

Calcium: 28 milligrams (mg) K is 303 milligrams (mg). 281 milligrams of sodium

Symptoms of Stage 1 Kidney Disease

A Salad of Roasted Cauliflower and Mixed Greens (see recipe #56).

PREP TIME: 10 MIN INGREDIENTS SERVES 4 DIRECTIONS:

TIME TO PREPARE: 35 MINUTES TIME TO COOK

Whatever you throw at mixed child salad greens, they'll handle it with ease. When combined with cauliflower, these lightly seasoned greens make a stunning display on a simple plate of mixed greens, with only one other vegetable taking precedence. Cooked until golden brown, the delicate cauliflower florets are accompanied by a light vinaigrette and a sprinkling of pecan pieces for added surface area and protein in this elegant supper accompaniment.

cauliflower (small head, cut into small florets): 1 cup extra-virgin olive oil, divided into 2 tablespoons peppercorns that are freshly ground

6 ounces of baby salad greens in a variety of colors. the walnut bits (about 2 tbsp.

Apple cider vinegar (about 1 tablespoon)

## METHOD

Preheat the oven to 400 degrees Fahrenheit.

Cauliflower and 1 tablespoon of olive oil are combined in a large mixing bowl. Pepper should be added towards the end of cooking. Make a single layer on a large baking sheet and arrange the orchestration.

Stirring occasionally, cook for 30 to 35 minutes, until delicate and brilliant brown, blending several times along the way. Allow for a 10-minute cooling period.

Meanwhile, combine the remaining tablespoon of olive oil with the vinegar in a small mixing bowl.

Mix together the mixed greens, pecans, and cauliflower in a large mixing bowl until well combined. Mix in the olive oil and vinegar mixture just before serving, and season with pepper if necessary.

Cooking tip: Make extra broiled cauliflower to serve as a side dish and keep some on hand so you can quickly whip up this plate of mixed greens when you're hungry. Three to five days will be sufficient storage time in an impermeable compartment of a cooler.

HEALTHY EATING DIRECTIONS

Caloric Value per Serving: 108 Glycemic Index: 9 grams

The following is the amount of saturated fat: 1 gram Zero milligrams of cholesterol 5 grams of carbohydrates 2 grams of fiber 2 grams of protein Phosphorus:\s42mg The following is the potassium content: 217 milligrams 50 milligrams of sodium

4th Stage of Kidney Failure

Salad de Bulgur et de Brocoli (57).

TIME TO PREPARE FOR SERVES 4: 10 MIN 15 MINUTES FOR THE COOKING

Despite the fact that mint is playing a supporting role here, this refreshing spice brings out the best in everything it comes into contact with. Here, the mint is combined with lemon, broccoli, and cherry tomatoes to create a vibrantly seasoned serving of mixed greens, which is anchored by nutty-tasting bulgur. Serve this plate of mixed greens on its own or spoon it into a salad dressing.

Make a delectable active plate of mixed greens wrap with colossal lettuce leaves.

INGREDIENTS

3-cups of chopped broccoli florets 1 cup of chopped cauliflower

Bulgur in a cup

2 cherry tomatoes, halved (12 cup total)

sunflower seeds (raw) in a quarter cup

chopped mint leaves (about a quarter cup) a lemon (with its juice) the extra-virgin olive oil (one tablespoon)

## METHOD

Fill a medium-sized bowl halfway with ice and water and set up an ice-water shower in it.

Almost completely fill a medium-sized pot with water and bring it up to a boil. Trim and blanche 3 minutes with the broccoli. Toss the broccoli into the ice shower with an open spoon while maintaining control over the temperature of the cooking water. After approximately 3 minutes of cooling, channel the ice and water through a channeling machine. Separate the broccoli from the rest of the vegetables.

To prepare the bulgur, add it to the boiling water and remove it from the heat. Cover and set aside for 15 minutes. Create a channel in the bulgur by squeezing it with the back of the spoon to remove any excess water.

Toss the broccoli, bulgur, tomatoes, sunflower seeds, mint, lemon juice, and olive oil in a medium-sized mixing bowl until well combined. Make a quick meal of it. Repair tip: Bulgur can smell bad quickly, so buy only what you will use right away rather than letting it sit around. Check for freshness by smelling it before purchasing and storing it in the refrigerator if at all possible.

## HEALTHY EATING DIRECTIONS

Caloric Value per Serving: 156 6 grams of total fat

The following is the amount of saturated fat: 1 gram Zero milligrams of cholesterol Contains 24 grams of carbohydrates. Fiber:\s7g

6 grams of protein Phosphorus:\s101mg Potassium:\s315mg 21.1 milligrams of sodium

Symptoms of Stage 1 Kidney Disease

CPSIA information can be obtained
at www.ICGtesting.com
Printed in the USA
BVHW060458170522
637110BV00025B/170